# Pan Kapitan of Jordanow

Compiled by William Leibner

**Published by JewishGen**

**An Affiliate of the Museum of Jewish Heritage - A Living Memorial to the Holocaust
New York**

Pan Kapitan of Jordanow

Complied by William Leibner
Edited by Erica S. Goldman-Brodie
Cover Design by  Rachel Kolokoff Hopper

Published by JewishGen, Inc.
An Affiliate of the Museum of Jewish Heritage
A Living Memorial to the Holocaust
36 Battery Place, New York, NY 10280

Printed in the United States of America by Lightning Source, Inc.

Library of Congress Control Number (LCCN): 2018936707

ISBN: 978-1-939561-65-7 (hard cover: 212 pages, alk. paper)

Front and back cover photographs from the book.

# JewishGen and the Yizkor-Books-in-Print Project

This book has been published by the **Yizkor-Books-in-Print Project,** as part of the **Yizkor Book Project** of **JewishGen, Inc**.

**JewishGen, Inc.** is a non-profit organization founded in 1987 as a resource for Jewish genealogy. Its website [www.jewishgen.org] serves as an international clearinghouse and resource center to assist individuals who are researching the history of their Jewish families and the places where they lived. JewishGen provides databases, facilitates discussion groups, and coordinates projects relating to Jewish genealogy and the history of the Jewish people. In 2003, JewishGen became an affiliate of the **Museum of Jewish Heritage - A Living Memorial to the Holocaust** in New York.

The **JewishGen Yizkor Book Project** was organized to make more widely known the existence of Yizkor (Memorial) Books written by survivors and former residents of various Jewish communities throughout the world. Later, volunteers connected to the different destroyed communities began cooperating to have these books translated from the original language—usually Hebrew or Yiddish—into English, thus enabling a wider audience to have access to the valuable information contained within them. As each chapter of these books was translated, it was posted on the JewishGen website and made available to the general public.

The **Yizkor-Books-in-Print Project** began in 2011 as an initiative to print and publish Yizkor Books that had been fully translated, so that hard copies would be available for purchase by the descendants of these communities and also by scholars, universities, synagogues, libraries, and museums.

These Yizkor books have been produced almost entirely through the volunteer effort of researchers from around the world, assisted by donations from private individuals. The books are printed and sold at near cost, so as to make them as affordable as possible. Our goal is to make this important genre of Jewish literature and history available in English in book form, so that people can have the personal histories of their ancestral towns on their bookshelves for themselves and for their children and grandchildren.

A list of all published translated Yizkor Books in the project with prices and ordering information can be found at:

http://www.jewishgen.org/Yizkor/ybip.html

*Lance Ackerfeld, Yizkor Book Project Manager*

*Joel Alpert, Yizkor-Book-in-Print Project Coordinator*

JewishGen
**Yizkor Book Project**

This book is presented by the
Yizkor Books in Print Project
Project Coordinator: Joel Alpert

Part of the
Yizkor Books Project of JewishGen, Inc.
Project Manager: Lance Ackerfeld

These books have been produced solely through volunteer effort
of individuals from around the world.  The books are printed and
sold at near cost, so as to make them as affordable as possible.

Our goal is to make this history and important genre of Jewish
literature available in English in book form so that people can have
the near-personal histories of their ancestral towns on their bookshelves for themselves and for their children and grandchildren.

Any donations to the Yizkor Books Project are appreciated.

Please send donations to:
Yizkor Book Project
JewishGen
36 Battery Place
New York, NY 10280

JewishGen, Inc. is an affiliate of the
Museum of Jewish Heritage
A Living Memorial to the Holocaust

## Explanation of the picture on the front cover:

These children are the remnants of Polish Jewry. They survived the Shoah since they lived in hiding in Christian homes. With the end of the war nobody came to reclaim them because their parents perished in the Shoah. They continued to live with their Christian families and frequently partook in attending various church activities. Yeshayahu Drucker devoted himself to remove these children from their Christian homes and bring them back to Judaism. Some of these children were the only survivors of entire Jewish families.

The numbers that we see below the pictures are the numbers that Yeshayahu Drucker gave the pictures when he pasted them in his pictorial album.

The background for Jordanow is designed from a photograph that Rachel Kolokoff Hopper took at the Budapest Kazinczy Stret Orthodox Synagogue combined with a textured background.

Yeshayahu Drucker devoted a good part of his life to rescuing Jewish children from non-Jewish homes. Many parents gave their children to Polish neighbors for safekeeping during the war. Most of the parents perished in the Shoah. With the end of the war, there was no one to claim the children and they remained with the "adopted" Polish families. Following his discharge from the Polish army, he devoted himself to rescue Jewish children from these homes and restore them to their Jewish families or place them in Jewish orphanages. He was a one-man operation but saved hundreds of children. Most of these children reached Israel. They flocked to his home in Israel and asked for guidance and help. He listened to them in spite of the fact that he himself faced absorption problems. To his dying days, he was surrounded by the children he rescued. They paid final homage to this man who devoted himself to them and attended the burial cemetery.

# Acknowledgments

I would like to acknowledge the following people for their help, without which this book could not have been written: Avner Shalev, chairman of the Yad Vashem Directorate, Dr. Robert Rozette, Director of the Yad Vashem library, Mimi Ash at the Yad Vashem center in Jerusalem, Dr. Daniel Uziel head of the archive division at Yad Vashem. The entire staff at the library of Yad Vashem; Zvi Oren director of the museum at the kibbutz of Lochamei Hagetaot who provided photographic material for the book.

Special thanks to Mrs. Claudette Leibner for her patience in listening to the material.

Thanks to Emil Leibner who constantly provided technical assistance and helped to see the project completed.

Special thanks are in order for Erica S. Goldman-Brodie who edited the text.

We would also like to tank all the interviewed people and those that helped with our work.

William Leibner

William Leibner also wrote the following books;

The Nowy Zmigrod Yizkor Book
The Krosno by the Wislok River, Yizkor Book
The Zabrze/Hindenburg Yizkor Book
The Unlikely Hero of Sobrance, Slovakia with Larry Price
The Brichahh Organisation History Book
Pan Kapitan of Jordanow, Poland, Yizkor Book
The Yizkor Book for 13 Jewish communities in the Ukraine

William Leibner also translated the following books;

The Korczyna Yizkor Book from Yiddish to English
The Jaslo Yizkor Book from from Hebrew to English
Blood Stained Feathers from Hebrew to English

# Geopolitical Information:

Jordanow, Poland is located at 49 degrees 39 minutes North Latitude and 19 degrees, 50 minutes East Longitude.

Alternate names for the town are:
Jordanów [Polish]
Yordanov [Yiddish]
Yordanuv [Russian], Yordanev
יורדאנוב    [Hebrew]

| Period | Town | District | Province | Country |
|---|---|---|---|---|
| Before WWI (c. 1900): | Jordanów | Myślenice | Galicia | Austrian Empire |
| Between the wars (c. 1930): | Jordanów | Maków | Kraków | Poland |
| After WWII (c. 1950): | Jordanów | | | Poland |
| Today (c. 2000): | Jordanów | | | Poland |

Jewish Population in 1921:  238

BALTIC SEA

LITHUANIA

RUSSIA

Vilnius ●

POLAND

BELARUS

GERMANY

● Poznan    Warsaw ●

● Lodz

● Prague    ● Zabrze

● Krakow

CZECH REPUBLIC    ● Jordanow

UKRAINE

SLOVAKIA

250 miles

0

0    250 Km    500 Km

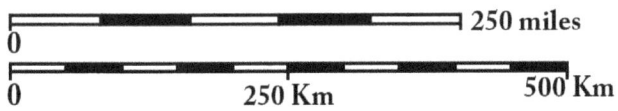

POLAND - Current Borders

# Notes to the Reader:

In order to obtain a list of all Shoah victims from Jordanow, the reader should access the Yad Vashem web site listed below; one can also search for specific family names using family name option. These lists are continually updated by Yad Vashem, so it is worthwhile to periodically search these lists.

There is much valuable information available on this web site, including the Pages of Testimony, etc.

http://yvng.yadvashem.org

A list of this book and all books available in the Yizkor-Book-In-Print Project along with prices is available at:

http://www.jewishgen.org/Yizkor/ybip.html

# Pan Kapitan of Jordanow

**Compiled by William Leibner**

# Table of Contents

Pan Kapitan of Jordanow

# Chapter I

# Jews in Jordanow
## (Jordanów, Poland)

### 49°39' / 19°50'

The hamlet of
Jordanow is south of
the city of Krakow
(Crakow in Polish)

Jordanów is a town in southern Poland, on the Skawa River. It was founded in 1564 by Spytko Jordan who received permission from the Polish king Zygmunt August to build the hamlet on the salt road from Kraków and Wieliczka to Orava and Hungary. In 1581 it received permission to organize annual fairs that became well known for the goods traded there, namely horses, cattle, linen, earthenware and salt. Spytko had great plans for Jordanów but he died and his wife barely managed the hamlet. The area declined in importance as it passed from one noble family to another. In 1772, Jordanów was annexed by the Habsburg Empire and remained in Austrian Galicia until 1918. During Austrian rule, the town's economic situation slightly improved with the arrival of the railway in 188, but Jordanów remained poor, with high unemployment and no industry. It became a center for Jewish summer camps for children who came from Krakow. It is estimated that about 5,000 children spent part of their summer in Jordanów, which had a favorable summer climate. The Polish government also tried to stimulate tourism by promoting the spa industry in Jordanów.

The exact date of Jewish arrival in Jordanów is unknown. Since its founding in 1564, the town saw many traveling Jewish, merchants mainly salt dealers, passing through the hamlet but they were forbidden to reside or deal in salt in the hamlet. Jordanow was close to the famous Wieliczka salt mines that provided huge amounts of salt for hundreds of years to Europe. Salt was a very expensive item in the Middle Ages. Jews were forbidden to deal in salt by order of King Zygmunt August. This did not prevent them from dealing with salt derivatives or supplying the mines and miners with their needs. With the arrival of the Austrians, these bans were removed as Empress Maria Teresa and later her son Joseph II greatly encouraged the economic development of the area. Jews began to settle in Jordanów and help the local economy, as the chart below indicates. By 1870, a small Jewish community existed. The exact date of the erection of the synagogue in Jordanów is unknown. Presumably it took place in the second half of the nineteenth century. The Neo-Baroque style is characteristic of the second half of the nineteenth century. Moreover, the official list of sacred buildings from 1870 lists the synagogue in Jordanów. The synagogue was located in the center of Jordanow. The synagogue was destroyed during World War II. The Jewish community of Jordanow also represented the communities of Rabka and Makow. The rabbi's title was Rabbi of Jordanów, Rabka and Makow. In 1887, Rabbi Israel Shramber was appointed rabbi of Jordanów and remained at his post until he passed away in 1929. He was succeeded by his son-in-law, Rabbi Elkana Zuberman. He remained at his post until Germany attacked Poland in September, 1939. He then left Jordanów, as other Jews did, and headed east. The Soviets sent him to Siberia where he remained until the Polish-Soviet agreement allowed him to leave Siberia and settle in Kazakhstan. In 1946, Rabbi Zuberman returned to Poland and became chief rabbi of Walbrzych or Waldenburg, near Wroclaw. He later left for the United States. There was also a Jewish cemetery in Jordanów that served several adjoining small Jewish communities.

| Year | Jews | Non-Jews |
|------|------|----------|
| 1880 | 80   | 1,236    |
| 1890 | 104  | 1,262    |
| 1900 | 158  | 1,345    |
| 1910 | 188  | 1,511    |
| 1921 | 238  | 1,486    |

## Jewish population in Jordanów through the years

According to the census of 1921, Jordanów was inhabited by 238 Jews, which made up 16% of the total population. The Jewish community was very religious and totally controlled by Orthodox elements. In the 1936 elections to the kehila, 300 voters participated, including the Jews of Rabka and Makow. The same year , A. Friedlich retired from kehila activities after serving the community for 50 years. 1936 also saw the creation of a "gmilu t chessed fund" to help the needy.

As mentioned above, the Jewish population of Jordanow was very religious. Zionism faced a tough struggle in getting a foothold in the hamlet. Israel Drucker moved to Jordanów in 1913 following his marriage to Rachel Tislowicz. He opened a jewelery store and tried to conduct Mizrahi Zionist activities. He was not very successful and returned to Krakow in 1914 with his family that now consisted of himself, his wife and his son Yeshayahu. Is rael's efforts were not in vain for Zionist youth movements began to appear in Jordanów. The big boost of Zionism came through the many summer camps of the Zionist youth movements. These youngsters spread Zionist ideas in Jordanow. In 1931, a branch of the religious youth movement "Akiva" or " Bnei Akiva" opened in Jordanow. It was followed by the Marxist-Zionist youth movement "Shomer Ha-Tzair" in 1935, Jews in Jordanów also voted for Zionist delegates to the Zionist Congress.

The German army attacked the Jordanów area in Poland on September 1, 1939. A sizable number of Jews including the rabbi of the town, Zuberman, left and headed in the direction of Lemberg. The Germans came from the south or Slovakia and headed north to Krakow. Heavy fighting took place between the Polish and German armies, resulting in a great deal of destruction in Jordanów. On September 3, 1939, the Germans occupied Jordanów. A unit of of German tanks entered the center of town and began indiscriminate shelling of the private houses in the center of the marketplace. Out of 400 houses, 270 were completely destroyed. The people who lived in the destroyed homes had to find shelter. The town would also be the scene of large-scale destruction in January, 1945 when the Soviet armies headed south to Slovakia. Jordanów suffered a great deal in 1939 and in 1945. It received the highest Polish medal, the Order of the Cross of Grunwald.

The Order of the Cross of Grunwald (*Polish:* Order Krzyża Grunwaldu) was a military decoration created in Poland in November 1943 by the High Command of Gwardia Ludowa, a World War II Polish resistance movement

When the Germans entered Jordanów on September 3, 1939, they began to persecute the Jews. Men and women aged 14 to 60 were conscripted into forced labor. Each day brought with it new orders and decrees that aimed at the pauperization of the Jewish inhabitants in the hamlet. Jews had to stop working their fields and were forced to surrender their agricultural tools. A ghetto was established where all Jews were forced to move. The Jews from the nearby villages were also forced to move to the ghetto of Jordanów. The Judenrat, headed by Erwin Kegal, was forced to provide labor for the Germans. Most of the workers were hardly paid and worked long hours building roads and rail lines. The Jewish economic situation was desperate. The

"Judische Soziale Selbsthilfe" or Jewish Self-Help Society ( better known by the initials J.S.S.) located in Krakow decided to open a branch in Jordanow administered by the local Jewish population. The branch helped the poor and needy Jewish population and opened a free kitchen for the needy. The J.S.S. was the only Jewish welfare organization in Poland that was officially recognized by the Nazi authorities. The organization helped the Jewish communities. The organization received great assistance from the Joint Distribution Committee.

Then the process of liquidation of the ghetto of Jordanów began. The Gestapo arrested the Feig family, who were American citizens, and shot them. Other Jews were also arrested and shot. Then the Germans demanded a huge contribution that was collected and given to them. On August 29, 1942, 400 Jews were rounded up in Jordanów and sent to the death camp of Belzec. During the roundup action, hidden Jews were discovered, and killed on the spot. Elderly and sick Jews were led to the cemetery and shot, while others were murdered in the district of Strzcze. Some Jews fled to the forests but were eventually hunted down by the Germans or the Polish police. Jordanów has no Jews today.

# Chapter II

# The Drucker Family

The Drucker family consisted of: Israel Drucker
                                  Rachel Tislowitz-Drucker
                                  Yeshayahu Drucker
                                  Aaron Drucker
                                  Dworah Drucker
                                  Yossef Drucker

**Israel Drucker** was born in Krakow in April 1888 to Mordechai and Miriam Drucker. The family was religious but saw to it that the children were provided with trades so that they could maintain themselves. Israel Drucker was trained as a watchmaker and worked at this trade. He later opened his own jewelry store. In 1913 he married Rachel Tislowitz, a native of Krakow. They moved to Jordanów where they opened a jewelry store.. Israel belonged to the Mizrahi movement and was very active in the party. The Mizrahi association in Hebrew: תנועת הַמִזְרָחִי, or *Tnuat HaMizrahi*, a synonym for Merkaz Ruhani or *religious center, was* the name of the religious Zionist organization founded in 1902 in Wilna at a world conference of religious Zionists called by Rabbi Yitzchak Yaacov Reines. Bnei Akiva, which was founded in 1929, is the youth movement associated with Mizrahi. Both Mizrahi and the Bnei Akiva youth movement are still international movements.

Mizrahi believes that the Torah should be at the center of Zionism and also sees Jewish nationalism as a means of achieving religious objectives. The Mizrahi Party was the first official religious Zionist party and founded the Ministry of Religious Affairs in Israel.. It pushed for laws enforcing kashrut and the observance of the Sabbath in the workplace. It also played a role prior to the creation of the State of Israel, building a network of religious schools that exist to this day, and took part in the political life of the Jewish people. The Mizrahi movement and the Bnei Akiva youth movements were very active in Poland.

Israel Drucker did not feel at ease in Jordanów and in 1914 moved back to Krakow. He was soon drafted by the Imperial Austrian Army and served four years. He was discharged with the end of World War I and had to start his business afresh. Slowly, step-by-step, he rebuilt his jewelry business in Krakow and the family regained economic security. Israel Drucker always hoped to settle some day in Palestine but, meanwhile, he had to support his family. He continued to support the Mizrahi Zionist movement and instilled a love of Zionism among his children.

Drucker saw the rise of Hitler in Germany and Hitler's speeches on the radio frightened him. As mentioned previously, Drucker served in the Austrian army and knew German. As the German menace grew, he was determined to run. This conviction was reinforced when Israel met a cousin of his from Berlin, Germany. The man was a very successful businessman and one day was ordered to leave Germany as a Polish citizen. The German police came to the house at night and presented an expulsion order. The police ordered him to get dressed ,packed and they rushed him to the rail station for the train that took him to the hamlet of Zbaszyn on the Polish side of the border between Poland and Germany. Of course, he was not the only one affected by this order.

Expulsions took place all over the Reich, but the actions conducted by the police differed from location to location. Most often, only the head of the family was expelled, but, sometimes, whole families were deported. The deportees were taken by train to the Polish border, usually in the vicinity of Zbaszyn and Beuthen. The Germans estimated that some seventeen thousand Jews were deported, but the precise figure may never be known. Among the deportees were elderly people, some who died during the journey. There were also cases of suicide and many of those who made it across the border had to be treated in the hospital. One of the Jewish families caught up in this *aktion* was the Grynszpan family from Hanover, Germany. The father, Zindel Grynszpan, later recalled the deportation: "On Thursday, October 27,1938, at 8 PM a policeman came and told me to come to Region II. Furthermore, he said, 'You are going to be back immediately, so do not pack but take your passports.' When he reached Region II , he saw a large number of people sitting, standing and crying. The S.S. were shouting, 'Sign, Sign, Sign the papers and we signed.' Gershon Silber refused to sign the statement and was placed in a corner where he remained standing for 24 hours.

There were about 600 people who stood in a concert hall the entire night. They were then sent by police trucks to the station where a train took them to the German-Polish border. Trains from all over Germany arrived and evicted Polish Jews. Of course, the Germans searched everybody and confiscated everything except for ten marks. This was the sum the Jews were allowed to take with them. Then the German police began to push and shove the Jews across the border. The Polish authorities did not anticipate the mass arrivals and pandemonium broke loose. Total confusion. The Poles permitted the refugees to cross the border but did not give them permission to leave the border area. Hunger, misery and hopelessness was the lot of these Jews when a truck with bread arrived from Poznan. Obviously, there was not enough bread for everybody and, again, chaos ensued.

**Jews with Polish citizenship being deported from Germany to Zbasz**

Zindel Grynszpan sent a postcard to his son Herschel in Paris, describing the horrors his family had experienced. Herschel, enraged at the treatment that his family and others suffered at the hands of the Germans, decided to seek revenge. He shot the German diplomat Ernst vom Rath in Paris. Vom Rath died as a result of his wounds. The Nazis in Germany used this as a pretext to launch the *Kristallnacht or Broken Glass* pogrom that saw synagogues and businesses burnt and looted, Jews murdered or incarcerated in concentration camps.

For the refugees stranded on the Polish side of the German/Polish border, help arrived from Warsaw on the afternoon of October 30, 1938, supplied by Emanuel Ringelblum and Yitzhak Gitterman of the Joint Distribution Committee or JDC. They established the General Jewish Aid Committee for Jewish Refugees from Germany in Poland.

**Ernst vom Rath**

A committee to help the refugees was also set up in Zbaszyn, headed by a Jewish flour-mill owner named Grzybowski.

Israel Drucker's relative managed to enter Poland and met Israel. He described in greater detail what had taken place in Germany and at the German border. The relative remained a short spell in Poland and managed to obtain a visa to enter the United States..

Israel Drucker was determined not to stay under German rule. He kept saying: "Where Hitler rules, there is no room for Jews." Furthemore,Israel said, "I shall never live under German rule." Many Jews were favorably disposed to Germany and remembered the Germans during World War I when German soldiers maintained order in Krakow. But Israel heard and saw the new Germany. When Germany attacked Poland on September 1, 1939[1], he made up his mind to head east. He closed his jewelry stores located at Nostrawa Street and at Dluga Street in Krakow. He started on foot on Sunday, September 3, 1939. The group consisted of Israel Drucker, his wife Rachel, his sons; Yeshayahu, Aaron and Yossef, his daughter Dworah and Riwkah

Luftglass sister of Rachel Drucker. Riwka's husband, Zvi Luftglas and their son Yeshahyu Luftglass.

Israel Drucker led the group to the eastern border of Poland. At first the group walked, then Israel hired a horse and buggy. After a week of walking and traveling, Rachel Drucker, her daughter Dworah, Rachel's sister Riwka and her family decided to return to Krakow. They were tired and saw no hope in these wanderings. Besides, the Germans treated women slightly better than men; even Jewish Polish women were left alone in Germany during the *Kristallnacht* pogrom. Israel however was determined to continue to move east with his sons[2]. Yossef Drucker was lost along the way and it took a great deal of time to find him. The Druckers continued to move on foot while the German army was on the move. Israel Drucker had a sister who lived in Kowel, which was part of Poland. He hoped to reach the city and then cross to nearby Vilna. Once in Vilna he hoped to find a way to get to Lithuania that was then free of Germans. He did not realize that during his wanderings, borders had changed.

On September 19,1939, Vilna was seized by the Soviet Union, which had invaded Poland two days earlier on September 17, 1939. On October 28, 1939, the Soviet Union handed over Vilna to Lithuania, which renamed the city Vilnius. Then the Soviet Union annexed Vilnius and Lithuania and created a Lithuanian Soviet government with Vilnius as the capital. Israel Drucker was not aware of these changes and continued to plot his way until he reached the Polish city of Kowel where his sister lived. He was well received and began to make contacts to cross the border to Vilnius that was now in Lithuania, free of Germans.

A smuggler was hired and the illegal journey began on December 31, 1939[3]. The night was very cloudy and foggy. One could barely see. Israel and his son Yossef moved close to the smuggler while Yeshayahu and his brother Aaron missed a turn. Contact was lost, the two brothers were separated from the smuggler who apparently kept going in order to cross the border. Yeshayahu and Aaron were lost and meandered back and forth but could not find the smuggler. The night was bitter cold and they decided to stop at the first farmhouse that they encountered. Meanwhile, the smuggler continued to move ahead and entered Lithuania. Israel Drucker and Yossef Drucker reached Vilnius. There was no possibility of leaving Lithuania and father and son remained in Vilnius where they perished together with the Jews of Lithuania.

**Yad Vashem Page of Testimony for Israel Drucker**
**submitted by his son**
**Yeshayahu Drucker. Dated May 20, 1990. Place of death:**
**Wilno, Lithuania.**

**Rachel Tislowicz-Drucker** was born in Krakow in 1889 to Yeshayahu and Yenta Tislowitz. She married Israel Drucker in Jordanów in 1913 and returned to Krakow in 1914. Israel was drafted in 1914 and Rachel had to support her family. She was a seamstress and managed to keep the family going until her husband returned from the army at the end of World War I. The economic situation of the family was very poor. The situation improved when Israel returned and opened a business. They eventually had two stores. Rachel spoke Polish and German. She returned to Krakow and opened one of the stores. She hoped that Israel reached his destination and would make arrangements for her to join him.

The German occupiers of Krakow soon started their anti-Jewish policies that led to the destruction and elimination of the city's Jewish community,. This has been vividly described in the movie, "Schindler's List," directed by Steven Spielberg. Rachel Drucker was sent to the Belzec death camp where she was murdered.

**Yad Vashem Page of Testimony for Rachel Drucker, submitted by her son Yeshayahu Drucker**

## Yeshayahu Drucker

Yeshayahu Drucker was the oldest son of Israel and Rachel Drucker. He was born in Jordanów in 1914. The family moved to Krakow where he spent his first years. He lived in the Jewish section of the city, Kazimierz. He started school at the Hebrew school where the language of instruction was Polish. It was called a Hebrew school because the Hebrew language was taught there. At a certain period of time his father transferred him to the newly established Mizrahi School. This school was totally different from the previous school. The Mizrahi School was modern and recognized by the Polish educational authorities. The language of instruction was Polish. Following four years of instruction, Yeshayahu Drucker's father took him out of this school and he returned to the old school that had an advanced high school academic program. The school population was Jewish as were all the teachers. The school was coeducational, boys and girls. The school atmosphere was very snobbish and Yeshayahu never made friends in this school. Most of the teachers at the high school tended to be anti-Zionist and assimilationist. Most of his friends were the students of the Mizrahi School.

Kazimierz was a historical district of Kraków, Poland. Since its inception in the fourteenth century to the early nineteenth century, Kazimierz was an independent city, a royal city of the Crown of the Polish Kingdom, located south of Kraków Old Town and separated by a branch of the Vistula River. For many centuries, Kazimierz was a place of coexistence between Christian and Jewish cultures; the northeastern part of the district was historically Jewish.

**Renaissance old synagogue in the Kazimierz district**

The area had very few non-Jewish residents. Yeshayahu came in contact with non-Jews in his father's store. He was never at ease with Polish Christians. At the store he talked a great deal with his father, to whom he was very attached. His father was a devoted Zionist and spoke Hebrew. He wanted to speak to him in Hebrew so that Yeshayahu would be ready to go to Palestine as a pioneer. The idea did not develop. The Poles who did come to the store bought or sold their watches or jewelry and left; very little social contact between the two sides. In general, he feared the Polish population and when his father sent him to Polish workshops or stores to repair or return items, He was terrified. Besides, Yeshayahu had no need of Polish friends since he was busy with the organization known as Hashomer Ha-Dati or religious guards, the forerunner of the Bnei Akiva religious youth organization in Poland.. He spent time with his friends from the early school days. Sometimes he spent a great deal of time at the clubhouse of the organization.

At the age of 14, his father started to look for a school where he could acquire an education to be able to support himself. The Hebrew high school that he attended was too expensive and he could not afford it. A cousin informed him that, in Warsaw, there was an institute to train Jewish religious teachers for the public Polish state schools. All Polish schools gave religious instruction to the children from which Jewish children were excused. However, the Polish government trained Jewish religious teachers to provide Jewish religious education for the Jewish children in the public school. The function of the seminar that was called the Feinslowicz Seminarium in Polish. This was a state educational institution with excellent and dedicated teachers, namely Janusz Korczak and Meir Balaban.

## Janusz Korczak

Janusz Korczak was the pen name of Henryk Goldszmit, born in 1878 or 1879, a physician, writer and educator. He was born in Warsaw, the son of an assimilated Jewish family. Korczak's father was a successful attorney who became mentally ill when Korczak was eleven. When Korczak began his medical practice, he did his best to help the poor and those who suffered the most, while at the same time he began to write. His first books, *Children of the Streets* (1901) and *A Child of the Salon* (1906), aroused great interest. Both as a doctor and a writer, Korczak was drawn to the world of the child. He worked in a Jewish children's hospital and took groups of children to summer camps, and in 1908 he began to work with orphans.

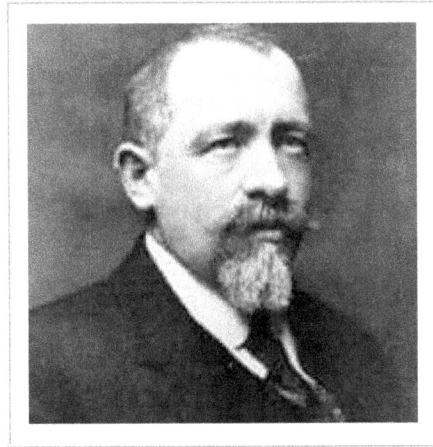

Meir Balaban, Jewish historian (1877–1942)

**Meir Balaban** was born on February 20, 1877 in Lemberg. He was one of the most outstanding historians of Polish and Galician Jews, and the founder of Polish Jewish historiography.. He received a traditional education at home and traditional Jewish schooling, namely the Hebrew language and Bible study in a *cheder*. He died on December 26, 1942, in the Warsaw Ghetto.

Yeshayahu Drucker left home at age of 14 and traveled to Warsaw where he was admitted to the seminar. The seminar was organized along years of study and was located in the heartland of Jewish Warsaw, Gensza Street 9[4]. The school concentrated on the study of Hebrew, biblical texts, Jewish history and the Polish language in order to be able to teach in the Polish public schools. The school population ranged between 120-150 students originating from all over Poland. Yeshayahu Drucker enjoyed the school and devoted himself to the studies. He remained at the school until 1932. He witnessed a decline of the Zionist appeal among the Jewish youth and the growing influence of the Communist ideology within the seminar. There was even a communist cell within the seminar that printed Communist flyers and frequently hid the materials between the religious books in the small synagogue of the seminar. Many students became Communist leaders[5]. Some even went to jail, since the Communist Party was illegal in Poland. Most of the printing of illegal material was done in the dorms and then distributed throughout the school Of course, the Communist students were not interested in the Jewish religion and did not intend to become teachers of Jewish religion. Most of them left school at the end of the third year. Yeshayahu continued for one more year and then left the school since he did not intend to become a religious teacher.

Yeshayahu was very active at the school and was a member of the student union that operated a variety of stores to provide the students with special needs such as paper supplies. The school even tried to encourage Yeshayahu to stay at the school. But he returned home and worked with his father at the store. He also began to prepare for the baccalaureate examinations with private tutors. To cover his expenses, he worked at many jobs including operating knitting looms.

Following the exams, he returned to the seminar and became youth coordinator of the Bnei Akiva youth group and student leader. In 1937-1938 he resumed a full study program and was also teaching at the seminar. The next year, he continued his studies and finished the fifth year of studies at the seminar. Many students then left to continue their studies at the Hebrew University in Palestine. He was still undecided as to his future and headed home to Kraków.

The city had a large Jewish population of about 50,000 Jews or 25% of the total population. Jews played a very important role in the city, especially in the economic and commercial sectors. All Jewish organizations had branches in the city that ranged from communist cells to the Hassidic courts. Kraków even had a Jewish representative in the Polish parliament, Rabbi Thon. He also officiated at Kraków' big progressive synagogue , similar to the Conservative synagogues in the United States. The head of the Jewish community was Dr. Moshe Landau, an assimilated Jew. There were many synagogues and Hassidic shtiblech or small synagogues in Kraków. Yeshayahu went to the synagogue that attracted the Bnei Akiva youth members. Krakow's secondary streets had many Jewish stores where the items were much cheaper than in the stores along the main streets. The latter stores were owned by Poles. There were some Jewish stores on the main streets but they tried to minimize their Jewish presence. The Jewish stores attracted not only city dwellers but also the peasantry from the vicinity of the city who sought bargains.

Yeshayahu Drucker failed his military medical test and was told to present himself again the following year. Even with the increase of tension along the borders between Germany and Poland, he remained at home. The government ordered ditches to be built in the city in case of air bombings. But life continued, the youth clubs continued to meet, the Jews went to their synagogues. And then on September 1, 1939, at 6 A.M.

Polish radio announced that German planes were attacking Poland. It even described the attacks and urged everybody to go to non-existent shelters. The next day was Saturday, and on Sunday the Drucker family left Kraków. The journey east led by Israel Drucker and the separation of Yashayahu and Aaron Drucker from their father is described above. The two brothers were lost and did not know where they were. The night was cold and they decided to enter the first farm that appeared.

## Aaron Drucker

Aaron Drucker was born in 1916 during World War One in Kraków. The Drucker family was in a poor state of affairs since Israel Drucker was in the army and Rachel Drucker could only provide a few pennies to keep the family going. Aaron went to cheder and then attended the advanced Hebrew school. He loved to manipulate mechanical gadgets and worked with his father in the jewelry store. He had manual dexterity and with time became an excellent watchmaker. He joined the family in the trip east. His technical skills would help them in Russia.

**Dworah Drucker** was born in Krakow in 1923. She was a student when the war started. She returned to Krakow with her mother.

## Yad Vashem Page of Testimony submitted by Yeshayahu Drucker for his sister Dworah Drucker, murdered at the Belzec death camp

**Yossef Drucker w**as born in 1925 in Krakow. He was an excellent student and excelled in religious studies. He leaned to orthodoxy and even became a devotee of the Hassidic court of Belz. He succeeded in reaching Vilna with his father. He remained in Lithuania and shared the fate of the Vilna Jews.

**Yad Vashem Page of Testimony submitted by Yeshayahu Drucker for his brother Yossef who was murdered in Lithuania**

### Riwkah Tislowitz-Luftglass

The sister of Rachel Tislowitz-Drucker, was born in Krakow. The two sisters were very close and even left Krakow together on the journey east. Riwkah was married to Zvi Luftglass, a native of Krakow. He was an engineer. They had one son named Yeshayahu. The two Yeshayahus, Luftglass and Drucker, were close friends. The Luftglass family left the family's eastward trek and returned to Krakow. The entire family was sent to the Belzec death camp where they perished.

2177

## רשות־הזיכרון לשואה ולגבורה, ירושלים

# דף-עד

### לרשום חללי השואה והגבורה

2168392

**יד ושם**

ירושלים, הר הזיכרון
ת. ד. 3477

| | | | |
|---|---|---|---|
| תמונת הנספה: | באותיות לטיניות | באותיות עבריות | 1. שם המשפחה |
| | LUFT GLASS | לופטגלאס | |
| א) רצוי תמונת פספורט / דרכון | | | 2. שם פרטי |
| ב) נא לא להדביק את התמונה אלא לרשום את שם הנספה בגבירה השני. | | 3 כי | |
| | | | 2א. שם משפחה לפני הנישואים |
| | | | 3. תאריך לידה או גיל משוער |
| | | 1885 | |
| | גם באותיות לטיניות | 4. מקום לידה (עיר ארץ) | |
| | KALWARIA | קלוריה | |
| חוק זכרון השואה והגבורה — | 6. שם אב הנספה | 5. שם אם הנספה | |
| **יד ושם** | דוד | גולה | |
| 1953 תשי"ג | 8. מקצוע | 7. שם אשת או בעל הנספה | |
| קובע בסעיף מס' 2: | סוחר | רבקה | |
| תפקידו של יד-ושם הוא לאסוף אל המולדת את זכרם של כל אלה מבני העם היהודי, שנפלו ומסרו את נפשם, נלחמו ומרדו באויב הנאצי ובעוזריו, ולהציב שם זכר להם, לקהילות, לארגונים ולמוסדות שנחרבו בגלל השתייכותם לעם היהודי. | 9. מקום המגורים הקבוע (גם באותיות לטיניות) | | |
| | KRAKOW POLAND | קרקוב | |
| | 10. מקומות המגורים בעל המלחמה (גם באותיות לטיניות) | | |
| | | קרקוב | |
| (ספר החוקים מס' 132, יום אלול תשי"ג (28.8.53). | 11. נסיבות המוות (זמן, מקום, וכו') (תפקום גם באותיות לטיניות) | | |
| | | נספה באושוויץ בגלל | |

---

אני, החי"מ בכרך ראובן _____ קירבה משפחתית או אחרת בן _____ דוד

הגר בכתובת בת-ים, רח' יוסף לוי 48 _____

מצהיר/ה בזה כי העדות שמסרתי כאן על פרטיה היא נכונה ואמיתית, לפי מיטב ידיעתי והכרתי.

מקום ותאריך הרישום בת-ים 25.5.1990 _____ חתימה _____

## "...ונתתי להם בביתי ובחומותי יד ושם...אשר לא יכרת"

**Yad Vashem Page of Testimony submitted by
Yeshayahu Drucker for
his cousin Yeshayahu Luftglass who was murdered
at the Belzec death camp**

## Footnotes

1. Yeshayahu Drucker, Testimony at Yad Vashem in Jerusalem. File # 10526, dated July 30, 1997. P.11
2. Ibid., p.12
3. Drucker, Testimony, p.15
4. Drucker, Testimony, p.4
5. Ibid., p.5

# CHAPTER III

# Residence in Siberia

The Drucker brothers, Yeshayahu and Aaron, were lost, wet, hungry and exhausted along the Polish-Lithuanian border. Aaron said, "Let's walk to the nearest farm and spend the night." The smuggler had given up on them and they had no choice. They saw a farm and entered it. The farmer greeted them and gave them food and a place to sleep. They paid him and asked him whether he could help them cross the border. He answered in the affirmative. The farmer then told them that he had to visit a nearby friend and when he returned he would help them cross the border. They waited in the house and the farmer returned with two Soviet soldiers. They told the brothers to follow them to the police station where they were frisked and searched. Everything was spilled on the table. The brothers told the Soviets that their parents were in Vilna and they wanted to join them.[1] They had heard from other people that the Soviets usually let anyone go to Lithuania without a problem. But they were not aware that the order had been changed as of January 1, 1940. The Soviet Union now no longer permitted people to cross to Lithuania. A policeman asked questions and they answered. The brothers were then told to leave the base. They left the place but were stopped by a Soviet officer who told them to follow him. He began a series of questions that had nothing to do with the border crossing. The officer then saw Yeshayahu's Hebrew Bible and was certain that it was a code book. This impression was further strengthened by the fact that the Bible had written notations along the margins. As a student, Yeshayahu had taken notes of the explanations given by his Bible teacher, Dr. Moshe Guliger, and entered them in his Bible, his favorite subject. The Soviet officer refused to accept the explanation and insisted that the written items were codes. Furthermore, he said, "I am also Jewish and I know what the Bible is all about but the writings are codes."[2] He ordered the brothers detained and sent to a detention prison in the hamlet of Aszmarna along the old Polish-Lithuanian border where the sanitation facilities were beyond description. The place was overcrowded and they were assigned places next to the night pail. Every prisoner who had to relieve himself stepped on them, especially at night in the darkness. The stench was unbearable.

The detention room was locked and they remained there for days on end. Then, the night investigations began. The same questions over and over about the "code book." There was no physical violence but the dragging from and to the investigation room via narrow corridors was hell itself. Questions, questions and more questions all in Russian while the Druckers spoke Polish. The documents were then signed by each individual without reading the Russian content. During their stay in this prison, they were given the opportunity to write letters to their family. They wrote a postcard to an uncle in Wilno and a postcard to their mother in Krakow. After three months of investigations they were taken to the train station where a special train with barred windows awaited them. The train took them to the city of Slutsk, in White Russia. The prison there was well organized; the cells provided room for three inmates. The food was also reasonable. They were condemned to three years forced labor without ever appearing before a judge. The friendly guards revealed this information to them. They remained in Slutsk for about three months and then were taken to the railway station where they boarded a train consisting only of prisoners. The windows were barred and the doors were locked. The train started to roll and kept rolling eastward. The trip was never- ending and took weeks. They crossed rivers, forests, mountains and valleys and the trip continued. Occasionally, the train was shunted to a nearby station for an army or express train and they then resumed their trip. After weeks of traveling, they finally arrived at some forgotten station where they left the train and boarded large river boats. They navigated the large river for days and were fed black bread, salted fish and drank the water from the river. They then left the river and headed on foot to their desolated camp called Krotoi in the Uktizemlag area of the Archangelsk region, very close to the North Pole.

The transport was escorted into the desolate camp full of barracks and buildings. They were all assigned beds and issued eating utensils. They were given supper and sent to bed. Lights out at ten oclock. Next morning, the transport was lined up and the commandant of the camp read the rules pertaining to the behaviour in the camp. He spoke in Russian which the Drucker brothers did not understand. Then the men were organized into labor brigades and marched off into the forest. They walked several kilometers until they reached a clearing site. Here they were explained their job, namely they all became lumberjacks. They were given primitive tools and assigned sections of the forest where the trees had to be cut. Then the tress had to be cleared of branches and cut to specific dimensions. The logs were then stockpiled.[3] This required a great deal of strength and experience which the prisoners lacked. These logs were piled on top of each other and formed sizable triangles of logs. In the spring, the poles that held the triangles in place were removed and the logs rolled down the banks to the river. They floated downstream to a factory that converted them to wood products. Frequently, the logs jammed each other and prevented movement. The prisoners were given poles and were forced to ride the logs to unravel the jams. Lacking experience, many prisoners fell into the water and had to be rescued by their teammates. Many accidents and injuries resulted from the lack of experience and primitive tools.. Many prisoners like the Drucker brothers were city folks who never did such hard work and for so many hours per day. The tasks assigned to each labor group were beyond their ability to finish during the day. They soon devised ways of cheating the daily ratio by shifting logs from previous days to the present day. Obviously, no one did daily inventories in bitter Siberian cold, or better yet, accounting was sloppy, carried out by people who could not care or did not know any better. Nobody really cared as long as everybody went through the motions of working. Everybody was looking for food, clothing, or for other needs that one had to get through a barter system.. Money was useless since no one could purchase things for there were no stores. The camp inmates or enemies of the Soviet Union as they were called were bartering slowly the things that they brought with them for food. The supervisors, all former prisoners but restricted to the camp did not particularly take an interest in their work. They were primarily interested in acquiring food and spirit. Drinking hard liquor was their favorite past time.

Conditions in the camp were terrible, lack of food, lack of medicine and harsh weather caused many prisoners to be sick The physical work drained the prisoners, who had to drag themselves kilometers to the work place and back. They received 600 grams of bread and soup barely sufficient for such physical labor. Many prisoners exhausted themselves became sick and died. The medical facilities were practically non-existent and the mortality rate amongst the prisoners was high. Sunday was the day of rest when the prisoners had to tend to their needs. Some prisoners worked their former skills namely barbers, tailors or shoemakers and earned a few rubles that enabled them to buy extra bread to keep going. Of course, there was a black market in the camp where prisoners and frequently officials bought and sold items that they needed. The camp was transformed into a trading post that seemed to engulf the entire country.

The camp officials stole everything they could lay their hands on and sell it. Of course, food was the hottest item. Every so often, the camp police raided places and arrested people and their merchandise. But the black market continued since the camp store or canteen had nothing to offer but pictures of Stalin and Lenin or books of Marx and Engels. These books were used primarily by ripping pages and using the paper to roll cigarettes. Some officials lived off the camp in a special section of the camp where the oppressive atmosphere was a bit freer. But they were not permitted to leave the camp area. They lived in small, poor and desolate places. Completely isolated from contact with Russia except for the official government messengers that the regional offices sent. These officials were were also watched and observed by the secret police who were everywhere and instilled fear in everybody, even in these remote areas. Of course the camp population knew that there were worse camps where one can be sent for violating camp rules and a number of people disappeared without leaving a trace. Indeed the camp population felt their situation was hopeless.[4]

The prisoners were constantly watched even in these remote areas where they could disappear into the Siberian air. There were forests everywhere but no chairs or tables or furniture in the barracks. Everything was done in accordance with the five-year plans devised in Moscow. These plans did not always consider the needs of particular places, such as chairs for the camps. The heating in the barracks was provided by the burning of wood. The summers were hot and literally millions of mosquitoes were busy attacking every inch of exposed skin. The lumberjacks had to cover themselves from head to toe. In the winters the temperatures reached -50°C. On such occasion all work stopped and they remained in the camp. The hot summer and the bitter winter cold made life very difficult. The production was very limited since most of these workers were under fed and exhausted. They lacked basic tools. The Druckers brothers managed to stay together. That made life easier to endure. As mentioned earlier, Aaron Drucker was mechanically very handy. His skills were soon noticed by the officials as he would fix machinery that broke down. The maintenance of machines and tools was very sloppy in the camps and they constantly broke down.

He began to repair and was successful. Word soon spread about him. As he moved about the various labor groups he came in contact with many Russian Jewish prisoners who were sent to the camps for various charges. They had families back home who sent them packages of food or clothing. Some of the stuff they sold and bought other items. They also needed the services of Aaron Drucker to repair items that they needed. They could go through channels and wait for months to repair an item or fix it within a few days. The charge was paid in bread, jam, sugar, dry fruits. The economic situation of the brothers greatly improved as did their food supply. The partnership soon came to an end.

One day, a Russian Jewish prisoner from another section of the vast camp came and took Aaaron to his place of work. The man turned out to be a mining geologist. They left Drucker's camp and entered another sub camp. This place lodged technical people that worked at the oil fields. They also searched for new oil wells. The camp had a great deal of tools, even sensitive tools that were scattered and in dire need of repair. The engineer gave him some items to repair. Aaron managed to repair some of the items and restored them to working condition. The engineer was pleased and informed him that he would be transferred immediately to this new sub camp. A policeman escorted Aaron to his old camp where he assembled his few belongings and left the lumber jack camp. He could not say goodbye to his brother who was chopping trees in forest.

Aaron was assigned to a nice room with a bed. The food was much better than in the old camp. The secret police was still everywhere but living conditions were much better The fact that his work was basically inside buildings already improved his welfare. Aaron was pleased with the assignment and met his brother whenever he could and brought him food or other necessities. The separation between the camps was strict and they had to get permission to enter each others place of residence.

The camp was huge and contained other sections, namely drilling sections for gas. These workers were better fed and received better housing. Many of the workers were Russians and included many Russian Jews. They were familiar with the Soviet system and also received food packages from home. The entire camp was watched and observed by the secret police who were everywhere and instilled fear in everybody even in these remote areas. The officials were merely interested that everybody should look busy, as long as everybody went through the motions of working, the guards were pleased. In reality everybody was looking for food or for clothing or for other needs that one had to get through a system of barter or exchange of goods. Money was useless since no one could purchase things, for there were no stores.

Yeshayahu continued to chop trees and clean them before shipping. The logs were cut and placed on movable platforms that tractors dragged to the edge of cliffs. The safety retainers were removed and the logs rolled down to the river. Yeshayahu decided to hop a ride one of the platforms. Apparently he fell asleep and fell off the moving cart. The next cart rolled over his shoulder. The tractor driver continued to drive. Nobody was there to help and he could not move. He was on the ground helpless when a huge dog towered over him. The dog did not bite but kept barking. Finally a policeman appeared and helped him get up. He could not walk so the policeman helped him and jokingly asked him, "Where did you want to run." They reached the infirmary and the doctor told Yeshayahu to go back to work, adding, "I know an artist when I see one." Yeshayahu managed to reach his brother and explained the situation. Aaron contacted some officials and received permission for Yeshayahu to enter the technical camp. He also managed to contact the head doctor of the camp who happened to be Jewish. A new doctor was assigned to the case and he gave Yeshayahu a note stating that he had a clavicle fracture and must rest for three weeks. The rest period was extended and Yeshayahu was removed from the lumberjack camp to a section where a variety of workers lived. People that did not work as lumber jacks could not stay in this camp. Yeshayahu managed to register for boiler maintenance course with the help of his brother. The technical camp had extensive drilling fields where the search for new oil wells was constant and crews needed all kinds of equipment, including boilers to keep the water pressure steady.[5] Yeshayahu began to work at this new job and was pleased; at last he was finished with lumberjacking.

Yeshayahu worked with the boilers for several months and then he was transferred to a blacksmith. The blacksmith was a Russian German who did not like particularly Yeshayahu because he made serious mistakes in hammering the hot metals. The two did not get along. The blacksmith had been sentenced to 20 years hard labor but his term was always extended under one pretext or another. Finally, the blacksmith returned Yeshayahu to the pool of workers at the camp. Yeshayahu worked at many jobs but never returned to the forest.

## June 21, 1941 Germany attacked Russia

On this day in 1941, over 3 million German troops invaded Russia in three parallel offensives, in what was the most powerful invasion force in history. Nineteen panzer divisions, 3,000 tanks, 2,500 aircraft, and 7,000 artillery pieces poured across a thousand-mile front as Hitler went to war on a second front. Despite the fact that Germany and Russia had signed a "pact" in 1939, each guaranteeing the other a specific region of influence without interference from the other, suspicion remained high. The German forces advanced very rapidly in Russia. The German tanks were unstoppable. Russian cities fell one after the other. Russian armies disappeared or were chopped up into pieces at an alarming rate. Russian prisoners of war were marched by the thousands to Poland.

Now everything was in short supply in Russia and especially in the camps. Everything was needed for the army. Still the German armies advanced rapidly through Russia to the gates of Moscow where the harsh winter, the excellent defense system and the exhausted German armies came to a standstill. The Soviet government abandoned all slogans and reverted to the national Russian slogan "defend Mother Russia". Even in the distant camps of Siberia, films were shown describing the brutality of the German behavior towards the civilian Russian population. Newspapers like Pravda began to appear in the camp. The Druckers understood the spoken Russian language since it is similar in pronunciation to Polish but the written Russian language was written in the Cyrillic alphabet. The government tried to enlist the entire population in the war effort even the enemies of the state. The general feeling eased a bit and people began to make an effort to help the country in the war effort.

**German tanks attack Russia**

Then the Russian papers carried the news that Russia and Poland signed an agreement. The Sikorski–Mayski Agreement was a treaty between the Soviet Union and Poland, signed in London on 30 July 1941. The signatories were the Polish Prime Minister Wladyslaw Sikorski and Soviet Ambassador to the United Kingdom Ivan Mayski.

**Polish prime minister
Wladyslaw Sikorski**

**Ivan Mayski, Soviet
Ambassador to Britain**

With the advancing German armies across Russia, the latter needed all the help it could get in the war. The British urged Russia to renew relations with Poland. The same pressure was applied to the Polish government in exile in London. The Poles resented Russia for its invasion of Poland in September 1939 when it was being attacked by Germany. Sikorski decided to overlook the treacherous deed and talk to the Russians. His aim was to reestablish contact with the Poles in Russia. It is estimated that approximately 2 million Polish citizens including 250,000 soldiers were in Russia. The talks also resulted in a military alliance that was signed in Moscow on August 14,1941. Later that year, Sikorski went to Moscow with a diplomatic mission (including the future Polish ambassador to Moscow, Stanis³aw Kot, and chief of the Polish Military Mission in the Soviet Union, General Zygmunt Szyszko-Bohusz). The military agreement called for the formation of a Polish army in the Soviet Union under the leadership of General Wladyslaw Anders who was in a Russian prison. All Polish citizens were granted freedom. Stalin permitted the recruitment of the Polish army in the Soviet Union and granted it freedom of organization and action. All camps received orders to release Polish citizens for army duty in the Polish army.

**General Wladyslaw Anders**

Yeshayahu and Aaron discussed the news regarding the creation of a Polish army. They wondered whether to join this army if given the opportunity. They wanted to go home and saw the army as a way out of the Russian prison. They feared that they may have to stay in Russia forever. They saw about them people who had been condemned for a few years and when the prisom term was about to end, the term was extended for one reason or another as was the case with the blacksmith. They saw an opportunity to leave the prison camp and head back home with a rifle in their hand. Of course, they had no knowledge of what was happening in Poland. They gathered that the situation was bad according to the Russian propaganda films that were shown in the prison camp. Since they arrived in the camp they had no contact with their family in Poland. They assumed that the Russian films exaggerated the bad situation, especially for Jews. Both brothers decided to join the Polish army.

They did not wait too long, when an announcement was made that all Polish prisoners were to report to an assembly yard. They were lined up and proceded to a medical office where they were examined for army duty. Those that passed the test were ordered to go to their barrack and pack their belongings and return to the assembly yard. Yeshayahu and Aaron passed the test and joined all other Polish draftees in the yard. They were then led to a special section of the camp and assigned to barracks. They were ordered to rest, no work details and to eat. They were given plenty of food. They rested and enjoyed their leisure, awaiting orders. Both brothers were hopeful that they would return to Poland and see some of their families. Most Jews had heard rumors that the Germans mistreated the Jews but the extent of the destruction was not known. Yeshayahu began to visualize his return to Krakow. Orders arrived and the Polish group was taken to the railroad station and off they went to the Polish military base.

---

## Footnotes

1. Drucker, Testimony, p.16
2. Ibid., p.16
3. Related by Jacob Leibner
4. Ibid
5. Drucker, Testimony, p. 22

**Chapter IV**

# The Ander's Polish Army

The Soviet Union attacked Poland on September 17,1939, while Germany had been hammering away at Poland since September 1, 1939. The Soviet Union entered the war without even a formal declaration of war. After 20 days of fighting, Poland collapsed. German and Soviet forces proceeded to the previously agreed lines of divided Poland according to the secret Molotov–Ribbentrop Pact, signed on 23 August 1939.

The Red Army, which vastly outnumbered the Polish defenders, achieved its objectives rapidly and took some 230,000 Polish prisoners of war. In November 1939 the Soviet government annexed the entire Polish territory under its control. Some 13.5 million Polish citizens who fell under the military occupation were converted into new Soviet subjects. The move was approved by popular elections managed by the Communist Party, the secret police and the army. Of course, the vote was overwhelmingly in favor of joining the Soviet Union. Then, the Soviets launched a campaign of ethnic cleansing that began with a wave of arrests and summary executions of officers, policemen and priests. Over the next year and a half, the Soviets sent hundreds of thousands of people from eastern Poland to Siberia and other remote parts of the Soviet Union.

The Polish government severed all contacts with the Soviet government. The Poles established a Polish government in exile in Poland that received recognition from Britain, France and the United States. This Polish government was bitterly opposed to the Soviet Union for what it did to Poland. Britain pressured the Polish government to begin to talk to the Soviets. The Allies wanted a united front against Germany. The Poles had to bend a bit to Allied pressure. After long internal debates, the Polish government in exile decided to talk to the Soviets. The head of the Polish government in exile, General Władysław Eugeniusz Sikorski, was in favor of these negotiations.

**Polish prisoners of war being led into Soviet captivity**

**Władysław Eugeniusz Sikorski, Prime Minister of the Polish government in exile and commander in chief of the Polish military forces in the West**

Władysław Eugeniusz Sikorski was born May 20, 1881. He was a Polish military and political leader. Prior to the First World War, Sikorski established and participated in several underground organizations that promoted the cause of the independence of Poland from the Russian Empire. He fought with distinction in the Polish Legions during the First World War, and later in the newly created Polish Army during the Polish–Soviet War of 1919 to 1921. In that war he played a prominent role in the decisive Battle of Warsaw (1920). During the Second World War, Sikorski became Prime Minister of the Polish government in exile, Commander–in–Chief of the Polish Armed Forces, and a vigorous advocate of the Polish cause in the diplomatic sphere. He supported the reestablishment of diplomatic relations between Poland and the Soviet Union, which had been severed after the Soviet pact with Germany and the 1939 invasion of Poland. However, Soviet leader Joseph Stalin broke off Soviet–Polish diplomatic relations in April 1943 following Sikorski's request that the International Red Cross investigate the Katyń Forest massacre.

Sikorski wanted to get some benefits for the captive Polish population in the Soviet Union. He did not trust Stalin but knew that he had no choice in the matter. Sikorsk was also the head of the Polish military forces in the West, including ground troops and some air force and naval units that fought alongside the British forces. He knew that the Soviets held large numbers of Polish prisoners of war and he hoped to reactivate them into a fighting Polish force. He knew that negotiations with the Soviets would be hard because both sides approached the matter with suspicions and were forced into it by the Allies. Sikorski favored rapid discussions in the diplomatic sphere between Poland and the Soviet Union and hoped to establish diplomatic relations between Poland and the Soviet Union. He flew to the Soviet Union and signed the Sikorski–Mayski Agreement of July 30, 1941 that resulted in the Soviet Union agreeing to invalidate the territorial aspects of the pacts it had with Nazi Germany and to release tens of thousands of Polish prisoners of war held in Soviet camps. Pursuant to the agreement between the Polish government–in exile and the Soviet Union, the Soviets granted "political amnesty" to all Polish citizens in the Soviet Union. All these former so–called enemies of the Soviet Union could now reside everywhere in the Soviet Union. They could also enlist in the Polish Army, which would fight alongside the Red Army against Germany. A Polish embassy was established in the city of Kuybishev and Professor Stanislaw Kot was appointed Polish ambassador. He immediately set out to organize the necessary machinery to establish Polish centers throughout the Soviet Union whose main function was to locate and register Polish citizens in the Soviet Union.[1] Most of the appointed directors of the Polish branches in the Soviet Union were Poles in spite of the fact that Polish Jews constituted a sizable portion of the Polish population in the Soviet Union. Some "tokenism" or Jewish appointments were made in minor capacities. According to Professor Bauer, about 230,000 Polish Jews resided in the Soviet Union during the war and 175,000 of these Jews returned to Poland following World War II.[2] These figures were ignored by the Polish administration in the Soviet Union when it came to important positions. Of course, there was always a Polish Jew in some position who could be displayed to the press, especially the American press, indicating full Jewish participation in the Polish administration in the Soviet Union.

On August 4, 1941, Stalin released from the Lubianka prison in Moscow Polish General Władysław Anders. The general was dressed in his full military Polish military uniform and was assigned new quarters. On August 14, 1941 a military agreement was signed between Poland and the Soviet Union that attempted to specify the political and operational conditions for the functioning of the Polish Army on Soviet soil. Stalin agreed that this force would be subordinate to the officers of the Polish and Soviet armies during winter exercises of 1941. On August 17, 1941 Sikorski appointed Anders to head the Polish army that was being formed in the Soviet Union. General Anders issued the first command on August 22, 1941.

Władysław Albert Anders was a general in the Polish Army and later in life a politician and prominent member of the Polish government in exile. Anders was born on August 11, 1892, to his father Albert Anders and mother Elizabeth (maiden name Tauchert) in the village of Krośniewice–Błonie, 60 miles west of Warsaw, in what was then a part of the Russian Empire. Both his parents were of Baltic–German origin and he was baptized as a member of the Protestant Evangelical–Augsburg Church in Poland Anders had three brothers, Karol, Tadeusz and Jerzy, all of whom also went on to pursue careers in the military. With Polish independence in November 1918, he joined the Polish Army and would serve it until the end of World War II.

**General Władysław
Albert Anders**

General Władysław Anders appointed, General Michał Tokarzewski to begin the task of forming the Polish Army in the Soviet Union. General Tokarzewski received the military base at Buzuluk where he set up headquarters and staff for the Polish Army. Another divisional camp was opened at at Tatishtyevo and one at Tock.[3] These camps began to receive many Polish recruits who were given physical examinations and if passed were recruited to the army. They came from all over the Soviet Union, especially from the labor camps, the "gulags" and the prisoner of war camps. At first the Polish army accepted all arrivals following a medical test. As the organization of the army proceeded, unwritten orders were issued to limit severely the acceptance of Jews to the Polish army. As a matter of fact, platoons that had a high percentage of Jews were ordered to undergo further medical which eliminated the Jewish soldiers. The rejected soldiers were chased out of the Polish camp and left to fend for themselves. Yeshayahu and Aaron Drucker arrived at the base and were immediately escorted to the medical office. Both failed the medical tests and were escorted out of the camp. They were not the only ones, it seemed that most of the Jews from their camp were rejected while the non–Jewish Polish candidates were accepted. The cleansing of the Polish army was in full swing. Very few Jews were accepted into the army, most of them were needed professionals like doctors, lawyers or Jews with excellent connections like Menachem Begin, leader of the Polish Jewish Betar or revisionist Zionist youth movement. The sizable number of rejects were standing and milling about outside the Polish camp when Soviet troops stationed in the vicinity arrived and began to chase them out of the area to the nearby city, of Syktyvkar, capital city of the Komi Soviet Republic,[4] Yeshayahu was a free man but with no job or place of work. He also did not have papers permitting him to stay in the area. He had a paper indicating that he was going to the Polish Army base, which was no longer the case. Both Drucker brothers eventually found work as tractor technicians. Aaron was really a handy mechanic. The wages that they earned did not permit them to live so they started to remove gasoline from the tractors and sell it on the black market. They also stole tin with which they repaired cooking utensils. These illegal activities enabled them to survive.

The radical change in the drafting procedure of the Polish Army occurred after Anders saw the statistics of enlistments, according to which 60% of the recruits were Polish Jews.[5] Ambassador Kot estimated that only 40% of the original recruits were Jews.[6] Both leaders decided to adopt drastic measures to reduce the number of Jewish Polish soldiers. Some were ordered to appear before new medical boards that failed them. Others were assigned to non–existing units that were later discharged. New Jewish recruits were automatically disbarred from service unless they were badly needed or had stature, such as Menachem Begin, leader of the Polish Revisionist Zionist party. Various excuses were given for this blatant anti–Semitic behavior, such as the Jews are softies, they are not Polish patriots, or the Soviets released the Jews from the camps before the Poles.[7] The Polish command permitted these stories to circulate throughout the Polish Army without taking effective steps to stop the rumors or the discriminatory practices. As time went on, fewer and fewer Polish Jews volunteered for service with the Anders Army. Most of the Jewish soldiers in the Anders Army were treated miserably and some endured living hell.

Below is a description of a Polish Jewish soldier named Meir Lustgarten who managed to hang on in the Anders Army[8] The testimony is not a pleasant page in Polish military history.

"I was accepted into the army without any difficulty. During the first stage of organization, many Jews presented themselves for enlistment. In the beginning, they were accepted without any difficulties and there was, in fact, a Jewish majority in the army. This naturally did not please the Poles who sought ways of getting rid of the Jews, or at the very least, of limiting the percentage of Jews accepted into the army. The Polish Command thus ordered all soldiers to appear before a medical board. During the examination, most of the Jews were marked grade 'D' for physical fitness and were released from the service. This occurred at the outset of the winter of 1941–42. Men were freezing from the cold and were nevertheless released. The Polish Army remained free of Jews – judenrein as the Germans put it. From then on, Jews were not accepted into the Polish Army – only Poles were accepted".

The Soviets and the Poles disagreed on many military and administrative issues. The Soviets finally decided to let the Polish Army leave the Soviet Union. The first major transports took place in March–April 1942 that consisted of 44,000 people, 31,500 soldiers and 12,500 civilians.[9] Other major departures took place during August– September 1942, when 70,000 people left the Soviet Union, 45,000 soldiers and 25,000 civilians. The total number of evacuated Polish military men was about 76,500, and the total number of civilians reached 37,500. Most Poles left the Soviet Union by train to the port city of Krsnovodsk on the Caspian Sea where they sailed to the port city of Pahlevi in Iran.[10]

The harassment of Jewish Polish soldiers continued even during the evacuation. Below is a report submitted by the Polish captain Dowiaglo who was responsible for the transport.

This is what he wrote:[11]

"Before the first units of the Polish Army left Russia, that is on 22nd March, 1942, 300 Jews of 'A' classification who had been examined by a Russian health board since the Polish committee was no longer functioning were sent by the voyenkomat (the Soviet War Office) to the place where the division was stationed. However, (the Poles) ordered them to return to their points of departure. Some of the Jews requested N.K.V.D. intervention and this in turn asked the Polish authorities why these men were not being issued with uniforms and why they were being sent back. The Polish authorities replied that they did not have enough railroad cars to transport them. The N.K.V.D. immediately supplied cars and faced with this fact (the Poles) took them to Persia but did not provide them with uniforms. At the port of Pahlevi, all the Jews that were not in uniform were told that they were free to go. Several Jews then approached the British authorities and asked them to intervene and it was only by command of the British authorities that they were all issued with uniforms and inducted into the army".

The cruelty exposed by the report is beyond words. How could officers treat their co- citizens in such a manners? The Polish Jews were lucky that the Soviet NKVD officers refused to co–operate with the Polish anti–Jewish games and forced them to accept the Jews. Even the British authorities in Iran refused to accept the Polish anti–human games. Of course, the Poles blamed everybody for the low number of Jews among the evacuees: the British put pressure on them not to bring too many Jews to the Middle East and the Soviets did not want to let the Jews go[12]. Everybody was at fault except the Polish Army that managed to achieve whatever it wanted. The Anders Polish Army had between 3,500 to 4,000 Jewish Polish soldiers. This token figure General Anders managed to get from an estimated Jewish Polish population of about 200,000 that resided in the Soviet Union during the war years.[13] The Jewish military force represented 5% of the total military force of Anders. He also evacuated about 2,500 Jewish civilians. Following the second major evacuation, the Soviet Union stopped all further discussions about sending Poles that remained in the country. Even some Polish generals, including Zygmund Berling, remained in the Soviet Union. The Soviets did permit Polish orphanages to send their children to Iran, among them the famous transport of Jewish orphans nicknamed the Children of Teheran.

**Jewish children from Teheran Iran arrive in Palestine**

The historic irony of the entire Anders Polish Army was the fact that they landed in Palestine among the Jews. The latter did not receive them with open arms for the stories of the Polish behavior to the Jewish soldiers was well known and well described. The number of Jewish soldiers in Anders Army in Palestine soon melted down to about a thousand soldiers who chose to serve the Polish Army to the end of the war.[14]

**Renaissance old synagogue in the Kazimierz district**

## Footnotes

1. Gutman, Israel, Jews in General Anders Polish Army in the Soviet Union, Reprint from Yad Vashem Studies, Vol XII, Jerusalem, 1977, p. 234
2. Bauer Yehuda, Flight and Rescue , Random House, USA , 1970,p.124
3. Gutman, p. 234.
4. Drucker, Testimony, p. 23
5. Gutman p.236
6. Gutman p.236
7. Gutman p.238
8. Gutman  p. 241
9. Gutman  p. 241
10. Sarner, Anders' p.118
11. Sarner, Anders' p.118
12. Bauer, Flight, p.123
13. Gutman, p. 241
14. Gutman, p. 242

# Chapter V

# Berling's Polish Army

Following the departure of the Anders Army from the Soviet Union, relations between the Polish and Soviet governments steadily worsened with time. The Poles kept asking what happened to the missing Polish officers that the Soviets took prisoner in 1939. Thousands of Polish officers were known to have been taken prisoners yet no one knew where they were. The Soviets kept giving evasive answers, claiming that they were investigating or checking on the matter. Months passed and still thousands of Polish prisoners–of–war officers were missing. The Poles began to suspect the Soviets of foul play. Early in 1943, the Germans released information to the effect that hundreds of Polish officers had been found dead in the region of Smolensk. They accused the Soviets of killing these men. The Soviets denied the charge. In Fact, the massacre was prompted by NKVD chief Lavrentiy Beria's proposal to execute all captive members of the Polish officer corps, dated March 5, 1940. The proposal was approved by the Politburo of the Communist Party of the Soviet Union, including its leader, Joseph Stalin. The number of victims is estimated at about 22,000. The victims were executed in the Katyn Forest in the Soviet Union, in Kalinin and Kharkiv prisons, and elsewhere in the Soviet Union. About 8,000 were military officers imprisoned during the 1939 Soviet invasion of Poland, another 6,000 were police officers and the rest were arrested were members of the Polish intelligentsia including doctors, lawyers, landowners, officials and priests.

When the news reached the London–based Polish government in exile, it asked for an investigation by the International Committee of the Red Cross. Stalin immediately severed diplomatic relations with it. All Polish offices related to the London Polish government were closed throughout the Soviet Union. The Soviet Union claimed that the victims had been murdered by the Nazis in 1941 and continued to deny responsibility for the massacres until 1990. To date, nobody knows the reason for the mass killings of helpless Polish prisoners in Soviet hands.

Stalin closed all Polish offices and organizations in the Soviet Union. He ordered all Polish officials who represented the London Polish government to leave the Soviet Union. All ties between the Soviet Union and Poland were severed. But the Soviet

Union had a serious problem: the Soviet armies were advancing to the Polish borders and he had no Polish government behind him. He realized that the Poles were not going to accept Soviet officials managing Poland. Stalin then ordered the Polish communists in the Soviet Union to form an association, which they did, calling it the Union of Polish Patriots (*Society of Polish Patriots*, Polish: *Związek Patriotów Polskich*, ZPP). This association became very active in the Soviet Union in 1943. In May, 1943, ZPP was involved in the creation of the first infantry division named the Tadeusz Kosciuszko division of the Polish People's Army under the command of general Zygmunt Berling. Kosciuszko was a famous Polish military man who even fought with the American colonies against Britain.

## General Zygmunt Henryk Berling

Zygmunt Henryk Berling was a Polish general and politician. He fought for the independence of Poland in the early 20th century. Later, he became the commander of the 1st Polish Army in the Soviet Union and played an important role in the post–war Polish government. Zygmunt Berling was born in Limanowa on April 27, 1896. He joined the Polish Legions of Józef Piłsudski in 1914. At the end of the First World War he joined the re-born Polish Army, and served as an officer until 1939 when he retired. He was arrested by the Soviets in 1939 following the defeat of Poland. He was released from prison and joined Anders army but remained in the Soviet Union. He was appointed head of the new Polish Army created in the Soviet Union.

**About 11,000 Polish recruits were gathered at a camp at Sielce near Ryazan, Soviet Union,in May, 1943 where they were presented with the Polish flag, the beginning of the First Polish Army in the East under the leadership of General Zygmunt Berling.**

As mentioned earlier, the second Polish Army in the Soviet Union was called the Polish People's Army. It was created in 1943 and headed by General Berling. He was appointed to head the army and received Stalin's blessings. He launched an appeal to all Polish citizens in the Soviet Union to join the Polish army and help liberate Poland.

Yeshayahu Drucker heard the appeal in a labor camp. As mentioned previously, he had been rejected from the Polish Army and found a job as a technician. He and his brother worked as tractor technicians until one day, all people without proper identification were arrested and send to a labor camp. The Drucker brothers claimed that they were Polish citizens but the commander of the camp told them to join the Soviet Army and they would be released from the camp. Both brothers did not feel like returning to another labor camp and decided to join the new Polish Army. They were immediately provided with train tickets to Moscow and given the necessary papers. [1] They appeared before a military commission that consisted of a Polish Jewish doctor and a Polish Jewish male nurse. They were soldiers number 81 and 82 of the new Polish Army and were sent to a place called Dibibo where the Polish Army began to organize. More and more Poles joined the army, among them many Polish Jews. Military training began and they were prepared for battle in the area of Lenino near Smolensk. While undergoing military training, Yeshayahu heard that the Polish Army was in the process of establishing a Catholic chaplaincy for the Polish soldiers. Yehshayahu wrote a letter requesting a similar office for the Jewish soldiers. He never received a reply.

לכבוד

הגנרל ברלינג

מפקד הדיוויזיה הראשונה על שם קושצ'יושקו

בצבא הפולני על שם ואנדא ואסילבסקה

דאר צבאי...

מוסקבה, ינואר 1944

מפקדי

אני החי״מ ישעיהו דרוקר, חייל בגדוד השני של הדיוויזיה, פונה בזה בהכנעה רבה למפקדי ומבקש שכבודו ידאג לי ולחברי היהודים שבגדוד שלנו, שנוכל לקבל שירותים דתיים הדרושים לחיילים.

נודע לנו כי כבר אושרו ואורגנו שירותים דתיים לחיילים הפולנים הקתולים, ואני חושב כי מן הראוי לספק אותם שירותים לחיילים פולנים בני הדת היהודית.

הגדוד שלנו קיבל פקודות להתכונן ליציאה לקרב נגד האויב האכזר, ורצוי מאוד שיהיה לנו רב, או לפחות אדם שיהיה אחראי לחיילים היהודים שבגדוד, שיזמן אותם לתפילה ושידבר על לבם לפני צאתם למלחמה.

אין לי ספק כי היענותו של כבודו לבקשתי תגביר את המוטיבציה ללחום למען מולדתנו הפולנית ותתקבל בהכרת תודה על ידי כל החיילים היהודים שבצבא הפולני.

בכבוד רב,

ישעיהו דרוקר

הגדוד השני של הדיוויזיה

**Letter written by Yeshayahu Drucker to General Berling's headquarters.** [2]
**Below the Hebrew text is the English translation.**

*"With Respect, General Berling, Commanding Officer*
*First Kosciuszko Division, Wanda Wasylevska*
*Polish Army January, 1944 Moscow*
*Commanding Officers*

*My name is Yeshayahu Drucker, a soldier in the Second Regiment of the Division. I humbly turn to my commanding officer to ask that he concern himself with my plight and that of my comrades, the Jewish soldiers in our regiment, so we are able to receive the religious services provided to soldiers.*

*We have come to understand that religious services have already been organized and provided to those Polish soldiers of the Catholic faith. And I believe that the same services should be provided to Polish soldiers of the Jewish faith.*

*Our regiment has received orders to prepare for battle with our cruel enemy, and it is very desirable that we have a chaplain, or at least a person who will be responsible for the Jewish soldiers in our regiment, who can lead them in prayer and speak to their hearts before they go to war. I have no doubt in the interest of your honor to increase the motivation of the soldiers to fight for their Polish homeland and to receive thanks for this from all the Jewish soldiers in the Polish army.*

*With the utmost respect,*
*Yeshayahu Drucker*
*Second Regiment of the Division*
*No reply was received from the Polish Army."*

While training, Yeshayahu Drucker realized that Yom Kippur was about to be celebrated. He organized the service and even published the announcement in the regimental paper. Yeshayahu conducted the services from memory. He was assisted by Moshe Schiff, another Polish Jewish soldier. Many soldiers showed up for the "Kol Nidrei" service. There were no reprimands for this illegal military action. Of course, the higher echelons, including Berling, decided to ignore the event. Berling was a member of the ZPP whose president was Wanda Wasilewska, a Polish writer born in Krakow and known for her left wing writings. The ZPP officially created a Directorate ("Zarząd") that slowly assumed the form of a government with full Soviet backing. It began to publish newspapers and publications, and created a Polish infrastructure within the Soviet Union that replaced the one created by Sikorski, which Stalin had closed. In 1944, ZPP formally recognized the State National Council (*Krajowa Rada Narodowa*) and was responsible for the formation of the Polish Committee of National Liberation (*Polski Komitet Wyzwolenia Narodowego*) that would in effect assume the role of the Polish government in the Soviet Union and would administer all matters pertaining to

Polish interests, including signing border agreements with Polish neighbors such as the Soviet Union and Lithuania. On July 22, the Polish Committee of National Liberation was informed that Berling was appointed deputy commander of the Polish Army in the Soviet Union.

Yeshayahu Drucker's regiment, part of the Kosczusko Division, first division of the Polish People's Army, went into action on October 12, 1943, at the battle of Lenino in the Mogilev region of White Russia. The entire division had started to train only four months previously and still lacked the necessary physical stamina for a well-oiled military unit. Most of the soldiers were former inmates of Soviet prisons, gulags and labor camps. They lacked ample supplies. But their motivation was high. At last they would face the enemy face to face. The division had a sizable number of Polish Jews. The battle plan called for a direct frontal attack. The flanks were supported by Soviet military units. At first, the attack went well, but on the second day the Germans recaptured their lost ground since a Soviet relief forces did not arrive. The Kosciuszko division held its ground but sustained very heavy losses. The division was withdrawn from the battle for rest and replenishment of the ranks. This was the first engagement of a large Polish military division against well-trained German soldiers.

Yeshayahu Drucker's unit was resting and recuperating when they were transferred to the city of Berditchev for further training. Berditchev was a typical Jewish town in the Ukraine before the war. It was frequently referred to as the "Jerusalem of Volhynia." The city had been home to Rabbi Levi Yitzhak of Berditchev, a prominent Hassidic leader, and to Rabbi Yitzhak Ber Levinzon, a famous advocate of Jewish Enlightenment.

**Big Choral Synagogue in Berditchev (pre–Revolution photo)**

In 1926, there were 30,812 (55.6%) Jews in Berditchev and in 1939 there were 23,266 Jews. The Germans exterminated the Jewish population of Berditchev during World War II. In 1944, Yeshayahu Drucker found one Jewish woman and her daughter in Berditchev who had survived the war in the city. The woman's father was a religious slaughterer, a shochet, in the city and had a Torah scroll at home that survived the war. [3] The woman gave the torah to Yeshayahu for the use of the Jewish soldiers.

Passover was fast approaching in 1944 and Yeshayahu approached Eduard Ochab, political adviser of the second regiment, with a request for flour to bake matzot and potatoes. Apparently Ochab was familiar with Jewish traditions and granted the request on condition that the Jews bake their own matzot. Yeshayahu organized a seder for the soldiers.

Edward Ochab was born in 1906. He was a Polish communist, social activist and politician. As a member of the Communist Party of Poland from 1929, he was repeatedly imprisoned for his activities under the Polish regime of the time. In 1939, Ochab moved to the Soviet Union, where he became an early organizer and manager in the Union of Polish Patriots. In 1943 he joined General Berling's Army as a political officer and quickly advanced in its ranks. In 1944, he was a member of the Central Committee of the Polish Workers' Party (PPR) and in 1945 he became minister of public administration.

The retraining finished, Yeshayahu's regiment proceeded to execute General Rokossovsky's military orders. Aaron Drucker was sent to an officer course to become a weapons maintenance officer. The two brothers separated and would meet after the war. Each Polish division was attached to a Soviet general. At this time, there were already many Polish divisions. Many of the officers were Russians but they claimed to be Poles. Yeshayahu Drucker gave them lessons in Polish. He became the political officer of the unit that explained the great problems to the Polish soldiers, namely that the Germans had killed the Polish officers. Yeshayahu also explained to the Polish soldiers the great shift of the Polish borders to the west where there was an abundance of coal.

Yeshayahu's second regiment was again on the move. Cities, hamlets and villages were liberated but there were practically no Jewish survivors. There was terrible destruction everywhere but all evidence of the Jewish community, such as synagogues or cemeteries, had been decimated. The front moved rapidly forward and soon reached the Bug River, the new Polish–Soviet frontier. The Soviet–Polish forces pressed on and liberated Polish cities where the Polish forces were received like heroes. Yeshayahu and the other Jewish soldiers found no Jewish survivors in the once predominantly Jewish places. The local Poles were not terribly upset by this factor and some even praised Hitler for a job well done. [4] All Polish forces rushed in one direction, to the Vistula River that crossed Warsaw, the Polish capital.

On August 1, 1944, the Polish underground, one of the largest paramilitary organizations in occupied Europe, launched a city–wide rebellion against the retreating German army in Warsaw. The leaders of the revolt assumed that the Soviet–Polish forces would continue their military advances. They were dead wrong. Stalin had no intention of helping the revolt led by the Polish underground and dominated by the Armija Krajowa that was closely connected to the Polish government in exile in London. Stalin ordered all Soviet military operations to stop in the Warsaw area. This decision gave the Germans time to regroup and crush the revolt. The Poles fought bravely but were no match against battle–hardened German troops who leveled Warsaw house by house, similar to the crushing tactics used against the Jewish revolt in Warsaw a year earlier. The Jews in that revolt had begged the Poles for weapons but the assistance did not materialize. Now the Poles were begging for help but the Soviet Union refused to listen. The fighting lasted about 63 days, resulting in thousands of

Polish deaths and the deportations of thousands of Poles to concentration camps. The Polish soldiers were furious but the Soviet command had given the orders. [5] Several weeks later, the Germans evacuated the city of Warsaw for fear of being surrounded by Soviet troops. The Soviet–Polish forces began to move and took the city. Most of the city was destroyed. The second regiment was ordered to move in the direction of Auschwitz. Yeshayahu Drucker knew it was a terrible place but did not know the real facts. His unit arrived at Auschwitz that had just been liberated by four Soviet divisions. Yeshayahu saw an empty place with huge piles of shoes and talitot; he took one talit for personal use and also picked up a small bag that contained phylacteries used for daily morning prayers. The little bag had an inscription; the phylacteries had belonged to a Rabbi Weiss from Budapest, Hungary. [6]Yeshayahu and the other Jewish soldiers now saw the full tragedy of the Jewish people.

The second regiment of the Polish army was selected to represent Poland in the attack of Berlin. The unit returned to Warsaw where Yeshayahu went to visit his old school but the only thing left was the road. The road in front of the seminary was paved with wooden blocks to reduce the traffic noise so that the students would not be disturbed in their studies. The entire area had been destroyed beyond recognition. He continued to march without paying attention to any point along the road. During a break in the march, Yeshayahu sat with some other Jewish Polish soldiers and saw the steps leading to the Vistula River consisted of Jewish tombstones that had been removed from the Jewish cemetery of Modlin. Yeshayahu was deeplymoved by the scene. Next to him sat a former leader of the Zionist youth group, Gordonia, in Krakow, who said "these stones are the reason that I joined the Communist Party in order to get some revenge." His name was Bleifarb and he became the head of the U.B. or Polish NKVD. Of course, he changed his name. He eventually had to flee Poland. Yeshayahu does not know what happened to him. [7] He was not the only Jewish soldier to join the Polish secret service.

Yeshayahu continued to march forward with his unit. On one occasion he was sent on errands for the unit and picked up a couple of hitchhikers. The couple talked among themselves in Yiddish. This was the first encounter that Yeshayahu had with Polish Jewish survivors. He dropped them off and they continued their journey. The unit helped liberate the women's concentration camp of Stutthof where there were Jewish women. But the regiment moved at a fast pace across Prussia. He already saw signs stating that Berlin was so many kilometers away. The race to Berlin was on. The second regiment reached a village named Neuzitzing and bedded down for the night. Suddenly an alarm sounded. Yeshayahu's unit was being attacked by a band of members of the so–called Werewolf organization. This was the name given to a Nazi plan, which began development in 1944, to create a resistance force that would operate behind enemy lines as the Allies advanced through Germany. The unit's commander Sinicki was away but his assistant Oshmilowicz directed the defense and attacked the gang. [8] With daybreak the Polish troops saw a number of dead bodies while the rest of the Nazis apparently escaped back to their base. The regiment received orders to advance to Berlin where fighting was raging everywhere in the city. Slowly, house by house, the city was being captured. Yeshayahu's regiment fought its way into Berlin and entered the city on May 1, 1945. Fighting continued for a few days. Then the Germans capitulated on May 8, 1945. The next day, the regiment received permission to tour the city. They saw the well–fed and well–dressed American soldiers while they themselves were underfed and poorly clothed.

Yeshayahu's Polish unit participated in the great victory parade in Berlin. They saw a procession of 700 German generals being led to detention camps for prisoners of war. The Jewish soldiers were very pleased with the scene.

The Soviets did not like the idea of fraternization among the various Allied forces and began to send their own military units to the rear. Yeshayahu's unit returned to the Polish city of Siedlice. With ample time on his hands, Yeshayahu toured the city and met many Jewish residents, some of the survivors from the camps and some repatriated Polish Jews from the Soviet Union. Yeshayahu received a letter from his brother Aaron Drucker who was in Czechoslovakia.

———————

## Footnotes

1. Drucker, Testimony
2. Kurtz. p. 19
3. Drucker, Testimony p. 27
4. Drucker, Testimony, p. 30.
5. Drucker, Testimony p. .31
6. Drucker, Testimony p. .31
7. Drucker, Testimony p. 32
8. Drucker, Testimony p. 34

## Chapter VI

# Drucker Joins the Chaplaincy Office

The Soviet and Polish armies were advancing toward Poland. The Polish government in the Soviet Union began to prepare to move to liberated-Poland. This government was only recognized by the Soviet Union. Stalin decided to publicize this Polish government. He ordered the release of Emil Sommerstein from the Lubianka prison. He was shaved, dressed and became a minister in the Polish government. This indeed was a first, because the Polish government in exile in London did not have a Jewish minister or assistant Jewish ministers. Jews were kept at a distance from the government just as they were kept between the wars. Sommerstein was not the only non–Communist in the government. Stalin wanted to attract publicity for his Polish government.

Dr. Emil Sommerstein, a minister in the temporary Polish government

Dr. Emil Sommerstein, born in the village of Chleszczewa near Lwow, was an attorney but devoted himself to Zionism and politics. Sommerstein was elected to the Polish senate, serving as a deputy from 1922 to 1927 and again from 1929 to 1934. He was also a member of several important parliamentary commissions. In 1939

Sommerstein was arrested by the Soviet authorities, underwent severe interrogations and was sent from gulag to gulag. Suddenly, he was shaved, showered, dressed and appointed a member of the provisional Polish cabinet, the first Polish Jew to hold such office in a Polish government. Stalin was determined to control Poland since he would need a bridge between the Soviet Union and East Germany where his army would be stationed. He decided to rehabilitate the once well–known Polish political figure.[1] There were a few other Polish non–communists in the cabinet, but the majority of them were Communist Party members or communist sympathizers answerable to Moscow. The appointments were well received in the West especially in the American press.

Sommerstein was familiar with Soviet political tactics and knew full well that he was being used for propaganda purposes. But he was also interested in re-establishing Jewish life in liberated Poland. This he could achieve by co–operating with the Polish government and the Soviet Union. He decided to play along and try to obtain as many benefits as possible for Jewish Shoah survivors in Poland and they needed every bit of help. He was also instrumental in the creation of the Provisional Central Committee of Polish Jews in October, 1944 under the umbrella of the PKWN or Polish Committee of National Liberation (*Polski Komitet Wyzwolenia Narodowego*). The PKWN was formed in Moscow from the ranks of the KRN, the Union of Polish Patriots (ZPP and the Polish Workers' Party (PPR)) This committee transformed itself officially into a provisional Polish government in the liberated Polish city of Chelm on July 22, 1944. It began to administer all liberated Polish areas. It followed Red Army units as they moved into Polish territory and expanded its authority within the Soviet-occupied Polish areas.

Sommerstein received money and launched the Provisional Central Committee of Polish Jews in October, 1944. The name of the Jewish organization was soon altered to the Central Committee of Polish Jews, also referred to as the Central Committee of Jews in Poland and abbreviated CKŻP (Polish: *Centralny Komitet Żydów w Polsce*, Yiddish: צענטראל קאמיטעט פון די ייִדן אין פוילן; or *Centraler Komitet fun di Jidn in Pojln*). It was a state-sponsored political representation of Jews in Poland. The Central Committee established Jewish community centers throughout liberated Poland and assisted Jewish Shoah survivors in resuming their lives in Poland. It legally represented all CKŻP-registered Polish Jews in their dealings with the new government and its agencies. Initially, a Provisional Committee of Polish Jews (*Tymczasowy Komitet Żydów Polskich*) convened in Lublin, chaired by Emil Sommerstein with Bundist Michał Shuldenfrei as Vice Chairman. Michal Shuldenfrei was born January 27, 1887. He was a lawyer by profession and an active Bund leader in Poland. In the interwar period in Poland, he served as a defense lawyer in several politically charged trials. During the last stages of the German occupation of Poland he joined the Soviet–sponsored State National Council. He was elected as the only member of the Jewish Bund to the 1947 Polish parliament. He reorganized the Bund in liberated Poland.

The General Jewish Labor Bund in Poland or אלגעמיינער יידישער ארבעטער בונד אין פוילין or *Algemeyner yidisher arbeter bund in Poyln,* was a Jewish socialist party in Poland that promoted the political, cultural and social autonomy of Jewish workers, sought to combat anti–Semitism and was generally opposed to Zionism. The Polish Bund emerged from the General Jewish Labor Bund in Lithuania, Poland and Russia of the erstwhile Russian empire. The Bund had party structures established among the Jewish communities in the Polish areas of the Russian empire. When Poland fell under German occupation in 1914, contact between the Bundists in Poland and the party center in St. Petersburg became difficult. In December 1917 the split between the two sections was formalized, as the Polish Bundists held a clandestine meeting in Lublin and reconstituted themselves as a separate political party later to be known as the Polish Bund. This party became the largest Jewish political party as shown by the Polish municipal elections in December, 1938 and January, 1939, before the start of the Second World War, in which the Bund received the largest segment of the Jewish vote[15] . In Warsaw, the Bund won 61.7% of the votes cast for Jewish parties, taking 17 of the 20 municipal council seats won by Jewish parties. In Łódź, the Bund won 57.4% (11 of 17 seats won by Jewish parties). Following the war, the Bund tried to reorganize the party and established branches in the main cities. The party opposed emigration to Palestine and tried to develop Jewish life in Poland. They usually played an important role in the Jewish communities and were well organized. They attracted the Jewish youth.

In February 1945, the Central Committee of Polish Jews was reorganized in Warsaw as the Central Committee of Jews in Poland. Its presidium included an uneasy coalition of

Jewish representatives who defined themselves as Communist, Bundist, Left and Right Poalei Tzion, Iḥud, He–Ḥaluts, Ha–Shomer ha–Tzair, the Union of Jewish Partisans, and the Jewish Fighting Organization. Emil Sommerstein remained the chair, with Marek Bitter, Adolf Berman (President 1946â€"1949) and Szlomo Herszenhorn as his deputies, and Paweł Zelicki as Secretary General. The CKŻP integrated local Jewish committees into a new multilevel hierarchy consisting of local, district, provincial and central echelons. It also appointed supervisors for local Jewish committees. The Committee created an Education Department headed by Szlomo Herszenhorn, an active Bundist educator who established the first Jewish orphanage in liberated Poland.

The Jewish Shoah survivors were former shadows of themselves.[2] They were afraid of everything. Their families murdered, their homes gone, they faced the hostile street alone. Sommerstein felt that the Jews needed a spiritual or religious uplift to get back on their feet. He saw that the Central Committee would not support the restitution of Jewish religious life in liberated Poland. He therefore insisted that the Polish government appoint a chief chaplain of the Polish Army to meet the spiritual needs of the Jewish soldiers.[3] There were about 13,000 registered Jewish soldiers in the Polish Army. Actually there were more Jewish soldiers but many omitted to state that fact for a variety of reasons and preferred to pass themselves off as Poles.[4] The army chaplain would also expand his influence in the liberated Polish areas since there were no rabbis in Poland. Sommerstein contacted Dr. Rabbi David Kahana in Lwow and asked him to come to Lublin where the Soviet–backed Polish government was headquartered.

The territorial changes of Poland immediately after World War II were very extensive. In 1945, after the defeat of Nazi Germany, Polish borders were redrawn in accordance with the decisions made by the Allies at the Potsdam Conference and at the insistence of the Soviet Union. The pre–war eastern Polish territories of Kresy, which the Red Army had invaded in 1939, were permanently annexed by the USSR, and most of their Polish inhabitants expelled. Today, these territories are part of sovereign Belarus, Ukraine and Lithuania.

The Government of the Republic of Poland in Exile also known as the Polish government in exile situated in London refused to recognize the new Polish borders and began a steady opposition campaign to the changes within Poland. Joseph Stalin was determined to implement the changes and since Soviet troops controlled the areas, the changes were immediately enforced. Stalin obtained full agreement from the provisional government of Poland or as it was popularly known as the Lublin government. After consultations with Stalin, Wanda Wasilewska, a native of Krakow, became the head of the newly formed *Związek Patriotów Polskich* (Society of Polish Patriots) in the Soviet Union. In 1944, she also became the deputy chief of the Polish Committee of National Liberation (PKWN). We already mentioned that these and other groups established the provisional Polish government that was immediately recognised by the Soviet Union. The Polish government in exile in London bitterly protested. The two Polish governments fought each other for recognition and legitimacy. Obviously the Lublin Polish government had the advantage since they began to administer the liberated Polish areas.

**Wanda Wasilewska**

The London exile government had the support of the Western powers and the Polish population in Poland. The Lublin Polish government brought Polish politicians like Sommerstein into the cabinet in order to boost its international standing. Sommerstein understood the game and wanted to gain benefits for the Polish Jewish Shoah survivors. He hoped that Jewish life would rekindle in liberated Poland but it needed governmental help, namely government financial subsidies that were granted to the Central Committee of Polish Jews. He also felt that a religious stimulus would strengthen the Jewish community. At present there was no Jewish religious authority in Poland. Sommerstein pushed for the establishment of a military Jewish chaplaincy office for the Polish armed forces[5]. He correctly assumed that the chief chaplain would become the spokesman for religious Polish Judaism. He selected Rabbi David Kahana to be the chief chaplain and invited him to Lublin where the Polish government was headquartered.

Rabbi Kahana was born in Chlamowka in the district of Tarnopol, Galicia, in 1903. He studied in Vienna where he was ordained as a rabbi and received a doctorate. In 1930, he became rabbi at the Sikstoska Synagogue in Lemberg several years prior to World War II. He survived the war and with the liberation of the area opened the first synagogue and also was appointed librarian to the Jewish section of the city library in Lemberg. He was a popular rabbi and was well accepted by the Polish Army. Furthermore, he had never left Polish soil and thus he was not tainted with any connections to the Soviet Union.

**Rabbi Dr. Major David Kahane in his military uniform with his family**

Sommerstein invited Rabbi Kahana to escort him to a meeting with the Polish prime minister, Edward Osobka–Morawski, and the minister of defense, Marshal Michal Rola Zymierski in Lublin on November 15, 1944.[6]Rabbi Kahana was appointed chief chaplain of the Polish Army with the rank of major. He was also granted a car, an office consisting of two chaplains, a cantor, a driver and a maintenance man.

Rabbi Kahana insisted that his office be granted permission to restore Jewish religious life in liberated Poland. Both Rabbi Kahana and Sommerstein knew that this was a difficult request since the government was predominantly communist and did not care about religion. But the Polish government wanted good publicity and indeed it was good tactics to show the Polish government helping Jews in Poland as opposed to the anti–Semitic Polish government in London. Rabbi Kahana was granted his request. The rabbi appointed Aaron Becker to begin visiting the renewed Jewish communities and help restore religious life by helping to organize synagogue services and providing the synagogues with religious articles including talitot and prayer books. These items were being collected by the chaplaincy office and distributed to the newly created Jewish religious associations in Poland. These activities were well received in the English–speaking countries.

The Central Committee of Polish Jews refused to cooperate with the Jewish religious associations. It had to tolerate their existence since this was the order of the government. The Central Committee did not contain religious or Revisionist representatives. Most of the members of the committee were unknown to the Polish Jewish survivors. With the addition of Itzhak Tzukerman and Tzvi Lubetkin as members of the committee, its status rose among the Jewish population.

The war was still raging in Poland and there were no other official rabbis. Rabbi Kahana became not only the chief military rabbi but also the rabbinic spokesman for Polish Jewry in liberated Poland. Thus, he represented Polish Jewry to the rest of the world and his office became the center of Jewish information in Poland. Furthermore, the Polish government authorized him to re–establish formerly destroyed Jewish religious communities in Poland. While the government was overwhelmingly anti–religious, internal and external politics required it to follow a path of religious reconciliation with the Catholic Church, the Jewish population and other religious groups. These political considerations only expanded the powers granted Rabbi Kahana and his office.

The Polish government's natural preference was dealing with the secular Central Committee of Polish Jews. This organization represented Jewish organizations and communities in liberated Poland.

**Yitzhak Zuckerman, Polish hero also known as Yitzhak Cukierman and Antek Zuckerman**

Yitzhak Zuckerman was born in 1915 in Warsaw, Poland. He was a hero of Jewish resistance to the Nazis in World War II and one of the few survivors of the Warsaw Ghetto Uprising. Zuckerman was active in a federation of young Zionist organizations, Hehalutz, and was an early advocate of armed resistance to Nazi plunder against the Jews. He was quick to interpret the first mass executions of Jews as the beginning of a systematic program of annihilation. Perceiving the full scope of Nazi plans and realizing that the Jews had nothing left to lose, in March 1942, Zuckerman represented Hehalutz at a meeting of Zionist groups and urged the creation and arming of a defense organization. Others feared that resistance would provoke the Nazis to greater violence. But on July 28, soon after the first daily trainload of 5,000 Jews had left the Warsaw ghetto to be gassed at the death camp of Treblinka, Jewish leaders accepted his view and created the Jewish Fighting Organization (Żydowska Organizacja Bojowa or ŻOB) under the leadership of Mordechai Anielewicz. Zuckerman became one of his three co–commanders and also helped lead a political affiliate founded at the same time, the Jewish National Committee (Żydowski Komitet Narodowy).

Zuckerman fought in the Polish uprising of 1944 in Warsaw and survived the war.

Zivia Lubetkin was also invited to join the Central Committee. She was born in Byeten near Slonim on November 9, 1914.

**Zivia Lubetkin**

She joined the Labor Zionist Movement at an early age. In her late teens she joined the Zionist youth movement, Dror, and in 1938 became a member of its Executive Council. After Nazi Germany and later the Soviet Union invaded Poland in September, 1939 she made a perilous journey from the Soviet–occupied part of the country to Warsaw to join the underground (ŻOB) there. She fought in the Polish uprising in Warsaw in 1944 and survived the war.

The executive committee of Central Committee consisted of 20 appointed men. It had an executive board of officers consisting of 8 members where the Zionists dominated, due to Sommerstein's influence. Later the committee was changed to 25 members; 13 members represented Zionist groupings and 12 represented the Bund, the Jewish Communists, and the Polish labor party. The head of the organization was Emil Zommerstein, a Zionist. The Revisionist and religious parties were not represented. The religious groups would be able to function under the aegis of Rabbi Kahana's office. The composition of the committee tilted to the left. This trend would continue. Most of the committee members believed in the idea that Jewish life should be restored in Poland. Most of them were opposed to the mass emigration of Jews to other countries. The committee began to reinstitute Jewish life in the restored and liberated areas of Poland. It established a child welfare department headed by Dr. Shlomo Hershhorn, a member of the Bund, who developed guidelines for the Jewish orphanages that were under the control of the committee. These guidelines stressed the Yiddish language, Yiddish culture, Jewish history and the official Polish school curriculum of the regime. These committee guidelines were sent to the Jewish orphanages that were being opened in many places. The stress of these institutions was socialist brotherly love and love of Poland under the new leadership.

Rabbi Kahana immersed himself in the task of restoring Jewish religious life in Poland. To do this he needed to hire a staff to implement his plan. When Rabbi Kahana received the letter of Yeshayahu Drucker offering his assistance he grabbed it with both hands. He immediately told Drucker that he knew all about him and promoted him to the rank of captain in the Polish army that would help him in his work. Rabbi Kahana informed him that he already had military chaplains. But he needed someone to join the chaplaincy in order to help revive the decimated Jewish religious communal life in Poland. Yeshayahu Drucker agreed to accept the position.

Yeshayahu began to travel throughout liberated Poland and wherever there was a Jewish community he stopped and helped the Jews organize the religious life that was decimated by the Germans. He helped with the official paperwork in the various municipalities. He always wore his uniform indicating that he was connected to the Polish state.

He took up residence in the capital and began his social service activities on behalf of the Jewish survivors in Poland. One of the survivors was Drucker's brother, Aaron, who had been discharged from the army as an officer. He married and resumed civilian life in Krakow. Aaron Drucker later left Poland for Israel.

———

## Footnotes

1. Bauer, Flight, p. 24.
2. Anna Cichopek–Gajraj, Beyond Violence, Cambridge University Press, 2014, p. 35.
3. David Kahane, Rabbi, After the Deluge, Jerusalem, Israel, 1981. Pp. 10–14. Hebrew
4. Cichopek–Gajraj, Beyond Violence, p. 44.
5. Drukecjer Tapes at Yad Vashem library. Hebrew.
6. Rabbi David Kahane, After the Flood, published by Mossad Kook 1981, p. 13.

## Chapter VII

# Drucker Activates Jewish Religious Communities in Liberated Poland

**Chaplain Yeshayahu Drucker with Jewish community leaders of Zabrze**

As mentioned above, the Soviet Army was not keen on seeing its troops mingling with American soldiers in Berlin. The Soviets ordered most of their soldiers out of the city except for special units. The Polish troops were also affected by this order. Yeshayahu's unit was ordered to report to the Polish city of Siedlice. The soldiers had plenty of time on their hands and began to sightsee. Yeshayahu met some Jews in Siedlice who told him about the Jewish community in the city that consisted of Shoah survivors, discharged Jewish soldiers and repatriated Polish Jews from the Soviet Union. They also told him that there was a chief Jewish chaplain in the Polish army named Rabbi David Kahana and chaplain Aaron Becker. This was news, for Drucker had never heard of these people while on active duty. He made further inquiries and discovered that the chaplaincy office conducted religious services throughout liberated Poland. He was also told that a bar mitzvah celebration was scheduled in the city of Siedlice with the participation of Rabbi Kahana.[1] Yeshayahu attended the ceremony and was impressed. He then wrote a letter to Rabbi Kahana in which he asked for more help for the Siedlice Jewish community and offered his assistance.

Rabbi Kahana replied that he needed another chaplain in his office. He also informed him that he would send his car to bring him to Warsaw. On the scheduled day, the car arrived and Drucker was driven to the office of the chaplaincy at 16 Allee Sucha in Warsaw, formerly the Gestapo headquarters in Warsaw. This was the residence of Rabbi Kahana and the chaplaincy offices as well as the offices of the Association of Polish Jewish Religious Communities. Rabbi Kahana enlisted Drucker as an officer with the rank of captain in the Polish Army. His major assignment would consist in helping restore Jewish religious communities throughout liberated Poland and provide them with the necessary religious articles namely, prayer books, bibles, and prayer shawls. Drucker's job would also consist of searching and locating rabbis that survived the war amongst the repatriated Jews from the Soviet Union and assign them to communities that wanted rabbinical help.

It would also be his job to help restore Jewish cemeteries and assist in opening kosher kitchens.[2] Chaplain Drucker accepted the position. Thus, Chaplain Drucker finished his active military career in August 1945 and began his career as a chaplain in the Polish army.[3] Rabbi Kahana also showed Chaplain Drucker the letter that he wrote to the Polish Army in the Soviet Union demanding spiritual guides similar to the ones that were established for Polish Catholics in the Polish Army.

Rabbi Kahana handed Chaplain Drucker a list of communities that he would have to visit and where he would conduct services during the forthcoming High Holidays. Drucker began to assemble the necessary materials for the communities and set out to infuse the surviving Jews with some hope and fortitude. The most important message that he carried was that the Jews were not isolated and hopeless. The chaplains were also busy preparing lists of Polish Jewish officers who wanted to retire from the army. These lists were then submitted to Rabbi Kahana who in turn submitted them to the Polish Minister of Defense, Marshal Michal Rola–Zimiersky. The latter usually approved the requests and some officers then left Poland while others retired to civilian life as did Aaron Drucker.

**A Polish synagogue being reactivated as a place of worship. Rabbi Kahana reciting a prayer while Rabbi Drucker stands on his left and the military cantor on his right. Notice the lit menorah.**

Drucker partook in many ceremonies of restoring synagogues, cemeteries, and kosher kitchens. The Association of Religious Jewish Communities provided the synagogues with the necessary prayer shawls, prayer books and other religious items. The Jewish Shoah survivors and most of the Jews who had returned from the Soviet Union had no prayer shawls or prayer books. Many Polish city administrations dragged their feet when it came to issuing permits for establishing places of worship. On occasion, the local branch of the Central Committee of Polish Jews tried to prevent the opening of Jewish religious institutions. The Jewish military chaplains frequently intervened and expedited matters. The appearance of military Polish officers had the desired effect as was the case in Walbrzych or Waldenburg.

The first Jewish presence in Waldenburg dates to about 1830. The Jewish population in 1880 reached 328. At first they did not obtain permission to establish their own community, and joined the community of nearby Schweidnitz. From 1862 onward, religious services were conducted in Waldenburg in a large hall and local Jews consecrated a cemetery in the 1860s. Finally, in 1878, the Jews of Waldenburg were permitted to establish an autonomous community. The community purchased a plot of land and proceeded to build a synagogue that was completed in 1883. A Jewish community center was built on the same site in 1920. By early 1932 there were only 220 Jews left; anti–Semitic acts were on the rise and eventually escalated into physical violence and, as a result, Jews started leaving Waldenburg. The synagogue choir was very active as were the Zionist youth groups, the local branch of the WIZO organization, and the Central Union of German Jews. Cultural and welfare programs were carried out among the Jewish community. The synagogue was torched on November 9–10, 1938; by 1939, only 24 Jews still lived in the town. The few Jews who remained in Waldenburg after 1942 were deported to the camps where most of them perished.

The city of Waldenburg soon had no Jews because the Nazis soon had established a concentration camp on the outskirts of the city. The camp was established in 1943 and would run to May 1945. The camp was a sub branch of the big concentration camp Gross Rosen that had about 100 sub camps. The Waldenburg concentration camp used hundreds of inmates to do heavy physical work. Most of the inmates were Jews and many others died of sheer exhaustion, starvation and sickness. The camp was liberated by the Soviet army and several hundred Jewish inmates were released from the camp. Most of those who were able began to walk to the city of Waldenburg. Some of the inmates were too weak to walk and remained at the camp until their physical situation improved. Those inmates who were able walked to the city of Waldenburg where they began to establish a Jewish community. They were soon joined by discharged Jewish soldiers of the Polish and Soviet armies. The city was soon transferred to Poland in accordance with the Yalta and Potsdam Agreements. The name of the city was changed to Walbrzych. The Central Committee of Polish Jews soon opened a branch in Waldenburg that provided social services to the former camp inmates and to the new arrivals. The Polish government also directed many Poles to the new areas and provided many benefits. Many Jews took advantage of these benefits and moved to Walbzych including the Leibner family.

**We know very little about the grave but it seems to indicate the hasty elimination of people prior to the end of the war; the grave was located outside the city of Waldenburg or Walbrzych.**

## The growth of the Jewish population in Walbrzych[4]

| Month/ year | Jews in Walbrzych | Jewish % to Polish residents | Jewish % to total population |
|---|---|---|---|
| XII 1945 | 1000 | 6.7% | 1.3% |
| I 1946 | 2125 | 11.5% | 2.8% |
| III 1946 | 3114 | 13.8% | 3.9% |
| V 1946 | 4991 | 14.9% | 5.5% |
| VI 1946 | 6883* | 19.1% | 10.0% |
| VII 1946 | 7666 | 20.0% | 10.8% |
| X 1946 | 8305* | 17.7% | 11.4% |
| XI 1946 | 9022* | 18.5% | 12.2% |
| XII 1946 | 9392 | 18.5% | 12.6% |

\* The numbers with asterisk are the arithmetic means of the figures given at beginning and at the end of the month in question.

My family, the Leibners, was given an apartment in a working class neighborhood, 39 Red Army Street, that had been vacated by a German family. The German population had been forcibly removed from the city and sent to Germany. The German family had left almost everything in the apartment. By the door hung work clothes indicating that the owner was a coal miner. We children tried on the hat for size and played with it. We also found albums with pictures of the German army on the march across Europe. There were several German books on a shelf. The apartment was moderately furnished and livable.

Many Jews who returned from the Soviet Union settled in Walbrzych. The Polish government, the local branch of the Central Committee of Polish Jews and the American Jewish Joint Distribution Committee helped in the absorption of the new Jewish arrivals. Many cooperative ventures were formed by Jewish craftsmen. Jews were hired by the various municipal offices, mainly in the medical field. There were plenty of jobs. Close to 800 Jews worked in the mine and glass industries. A Jewish school was opened where instruction was given in Yiddish and Polish; it had an enrollment of 170 children. Other Jewish institutions in Walbrzych provided care for 432 children. Walbrzych had a Yiddish library, a variety of cultural and sport clubs, and Zionist organizations that were very active, especially Zionist youth movements like the Dror, Shomer Ha–Ttzair and Halutz movements. The city also provided a large hall to be used as a synagogue (as mentioned previously, the old synagogue of Waldenburg was torched in 1938). The local branch of the Association of Jewish Religious Communities saw to it that the place was furnished and functioned as a synagogue. Rabbi Kahana came to the synagogue in Walbrzych and brought many prayer shawls, prayer books and kippot or head coverings.

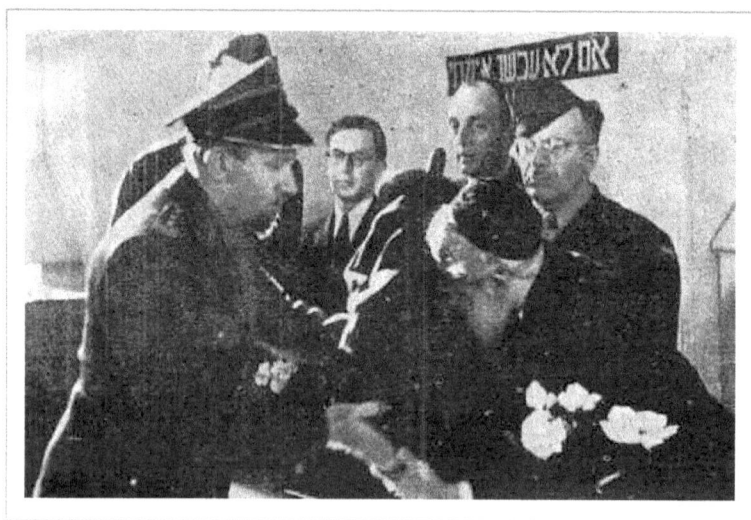

Rabbi David Kahana, chief army chaplain of the Polish Army (on the left) presents the chief rabbi of Palestine, Rabbi Itzhak Herzog (on the right) with a restored torah scroll. Next to Rabbi Herzog is Rabbi Salomon Wohlgelernter, head of the Vaad Hatzala in Europe (Yad Vashem).

My father and I attended the ceremony and I managed to get a small prayer book of my own. I could read the Hebrew prayers since Father insisted on teaching them but I could not read the instructions since they were in English and intended for American Jewish soldiers. Still, I treasured the prayer book for many years. The Association provided many religious items but there was a serious lack of torah scrolls throughout Europe. The chaplaincy office collected damaged scrolls and scribes were hired to repair, if possible, the damaged scrolls. Some were beyond repair and had to be buried in accordance with Jewish religious law while others were restored and given to the various congregations. The torah scroll campaign was very successful and some scrolls were even sent to Palestine where there was also a great need for scrolls.

Still, the Jews did not feel secure in Walbrzych. Every anti–Semitic event intensified our fears. Most anti–Semitic events were not reported in the press but spread by word of mouth. The fact that Jewish institutions had to be guarded by armed men indicated the seriousness of the situation. The head of the local branch of the Central Committee of Polish Jews, Jaacov Fishbein, tried to reassure the Jewish population that safety would be restored in the new Poland. Of course, he repeated the words of the Central Committee of Polish Jews that repeated the message of the Polish government. The reality was, however, different. The Polish countryside was vehemently anti–Jewish as were large segments of the Polish urban population. The Jews felt this mood and translated it by packing their things and waiting. The Zionists urged their members to leave Poland and head to Palestine. The communists, the bundists and the assimilationists urged the Jews to stay put and help build a new Poland. The head of the local Central Committee bitterly attacked those Jews who wanted to leave Poland. He sincerely believed in the new ideology of communism. Many Jews refused to buy into this policy.

My father was very active in the Ha–Poel Ha–Mizrahi or moderate religious Zionist movement. Meetings were held in our flat. Some young people even slept at our place. The discussions frequently revolved around going to Palestine or staying in Poland and hoping for the best. As time went by, I noticed that items disappeared from our flat. When I asked about it, I was told that new items would be purchased to replace the old ones. Of course, no new items were bought. Instead the family acquired backpacks and warm clothing as well as substantial amounts of food bought on the black market. Everything was packed and we were told that we were going hiking in the countryside.

We took the train at the Walbrzych station and headed to the country. We noticed that some other passengers had similar backpacks. We traveled a short distance and descended from the train and walked toward the forest. Father led the way and we followed. We rested in a small clearing where other people joined us. Toward evening, a few young men appeared and introduced themselves as Brichah agents. One of them spoke in Yiddish and said: "You are now in the border area. We will be moving in a single file. No talking, smoking or singing. Always stay close to the person in front of you. Within a short time it will be dark and we will begin to move." And so we left Poland.

**Members of the Zionist parties bought "Shekel" certificates that enabled them to vote for their party in the general elections of the Zionist World Congress. The shekel number 22467 was sold to Jakob Leibner residing at 39 Red Army Street in Walbrzych, Poland. The amount paid was 70 zlotes, Polish currency.**

We were not the only ones; more and more Jews in Poland decided to follow the Brichah call to leave Poland. Walbrzych was very close to the Czech border and served as a base for departure. Following the Kielce pogrom, the Jewish mass exodus from Poland began. Jews from all over Poland came to the border areas, including Walbrzych. They spent a short time there and even used the synagogue as a resting place before leaving for the border. The chaplains helped the movement of Jews by providing food and temporary shelter.

———

# Footnotes

1.  Yeshayahu Drucker's interview at Yad Vashem in Jerusalem
2.  Drucker Tapes at Yad Vashem in Jerusalem
3.  Drucker Tapes

**Chapter VIII**

# Yeshayahu Drucker Devotes Himself to the Zabrze Home

The chaplaincy office received many letters from Poland, the USA, Palestine and England inquiring about the whereabouts of their families in Poland. The next question that followed was: were there any survivors? The office replied if it had information. Many letters informed the chaplaincy office that some of their family survivors lived with non–Jews and asked for help and advice. The chaplaincy office was also frequently visited by local Polish Jews who asked for help in redeeming their relatives from non–Jewish homes. Chaplain Drucker saw this Jewish couple several times in the offices waiting to talk to Rabbi Kahana. Finally, the rabbi asked Drucker to see what he can do. Of course, Drucker had no experience in dealing with redeeming of children. Still he asked the couple to his office and they told him that a nephew of theirs is living with a non–Jewish baker. The couple talked to the baker but he did not want to let the boy go and the boy was attached to the baker. Drucker did not know where to start. He once had an experience with children in the city of Otwock near Warsaw. His unit received the order to search the entire town for German soldiers. They went from building to building, from cellar to cellar and searched for Germans. In one of cellars, they met an elderly Jewish woman with two grandchildren. The elderly woman was crying and stating that another grandchild was lost. Drucker went out of the cellar and began to look in the nearby streets for a small child. He noticed a small infant sitting on a stoop and crying. He asked the child why he was crying and he replied that he did not know where his grandmother was hiding. Drucker took the child and brought him to the grandmother. The reunification joy remained with Drucker for a long time[1].

Drucker asked the Jewish couple to join him and they went to meet the baker at the village of Wesola near Warsaw. The baker refused to give up the child who also refused to leave the baker. They returned empty handed to the capital. Drucker pondered various approaches to solve the problem. He started to visit the baker and appealed to his religious conscience as a man who had done a great deed in saving the child but now was acting in a selfish manner. He also stressed that the law was on the side of the relatives. After several meetings, the baker mellowed his stand.[2] Drucker then mentioned that the baker was entitled to some monetary compensation for his expenses in maintaining the child during the difficult years. These were difficult times in Poland where everything was very expensive and everybody could use some money. Finally, the baker consented to release the child. But the couple had no place for the child since they rented a corner of a room from another people. Drucker could not take the child since he was constantly traveling. There was one option, namely to take the child and place him in a home of the Central Committee of Polish Jews. Both Rabbi Kahana and chaplain Drucker did not like the idea of placing a Jewish child in these homes. Most of the Central Committee members were dedicated to the idea that Jewish life should be restored in Poland. Most of them were opposed to emigration of Jews to other countries. The committee began to restore Jewish life in the restored and liberated areas of Poland. It established a child welfare department headed by Dr. Shlomo Hershhorn, a member of the Bund, who developed guidelines for the Jewish orphanages that were under the control of the committee. These guidelines stressed the Yiddish language, and some aspects of Yiddish culture. No Jewish history, religion or Hebrew. Of course the official Polish school curriculum was followed at the homes. The committee guidelines were sent to the Jewish orphanages in Yiddish but they reflected the new regime. The stress of these guidelines was Socialist brotherly love and love of Poland under the new leadership. Rabbi Kahana and chaplain Drucker did not work so hard to place the Jewish boy in such a home.

The child had to remain with the baker until the relatives received a certificate to Palestine and took the boy with them. The boy was called Tulush; he maintained contact with Drucker. Years later, Drucker met the boy in Israel. He was now an adult and this is what he had to say: "My adopted father confessed to me on his death bed that my family name was Weinstein from Warsaw. He admitted that he was not related to me at all but he knew my family before the war. The couple wanted a child and invented the whole story of relatives." Weinstein maintained contact with the baker and his Polish family in Poland.

Rabbi Kahana and the chaplains realized that they must have a home to which the rescued children would be sent. A home was soon located in Zabrze or Hindenburg near Katowice. The building was originally an old age Jewish home for the aged of the community of Hindenburg. The building survived the war and was given to the Association of the Jewish religious communities in Poland. To maintain its original charter, the upstairs was reopened as a Jewish old age home and the bottom floors were reserved for the children. The building was part of a compound of the Jewish community that had several buildings, most of which survived the war. Unfortunately the synagogue of Zabrze was torched during the pogrom of the "Broken Glass" November 9–10, 1938. The building was totally destroyed as was the Jewish community a few years later.

**The Zabrze Jewish orphanage**

**The Jewish school of Zabrze on the left and the towers of the synagogue on the right form the Jewish compound of Zabrze**

A plaque was later erected in memory of the synagogue and the community of
Zabrze

**IN MEMORY**
**of the Jewish Community of Zabrze (Hindenburg) that was**
**destroyed by the German Nazis during the Shoah.**
**On this plot stood the Jewish synagogue that was built in 1872**
**and destroyed in the "Kristalnacht" pogrom of November 9–10. 1938.**
**" Remember what Amalek did to you on your way out of Egypt"**
**This memorial was erected due to the efforts of**
**Ernasta Shmuela Schindler and the community of Zabrze in 1998**

Rabbi Kahana requested the empty compound on behalf of the Jewish religious associations in liberated Poland. The request was granted in view of the military connections of the rabbi. The Polish army actually had a tradition of caring for orphanages. Even General Anders removed several orphanages when he moved his troops from the Soviet Union. So Kahana used all his connections within the Polish Army and obtained all the necessary permits. His moves infuriated the Central Committee that tried to control Jewish life in Poland. It had the support of the Polish government and the Communist party but it was facing stiff competition from the Association that was providing a host of religious services to the Jewish survivors without the need to be a member of the party.

**Director of the Zabrze Jewish orphanage was Dr.Nehema Geller**

Drucker received the order to get the building in shape to receive children. The Polish government and the Polish JDC were asked for money as were Jewish communities that were in contact with Rabbi Kahana. Drucker worked feverishly to provide the facility with all its needs. This was not easy, for the war had just ended and everything was in short supply in Poland. Dr. Nehema Geller, was hired as the director of the home. She was a Shoah survivor and native of Lemberg. Her husband Abraham was active in the in the Jewish community of Katowice. They had no children and decided to devote themselves to the needs of the Jewish survivors in Poland.

**David Hubel was hired as
headmaster of the school**

**Rudolf Wattenberg, gym teacher
and security official at Zabrze
orphanage**

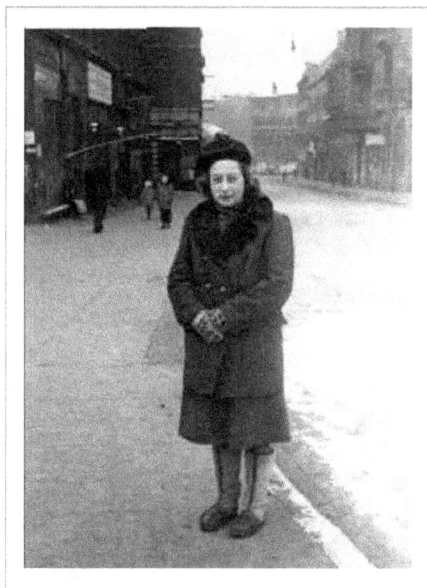

**Mira Katz took care of small
infants at the Zabrze Orphanage**

**Lucia was a teacher at the Zabzre
orphanage**

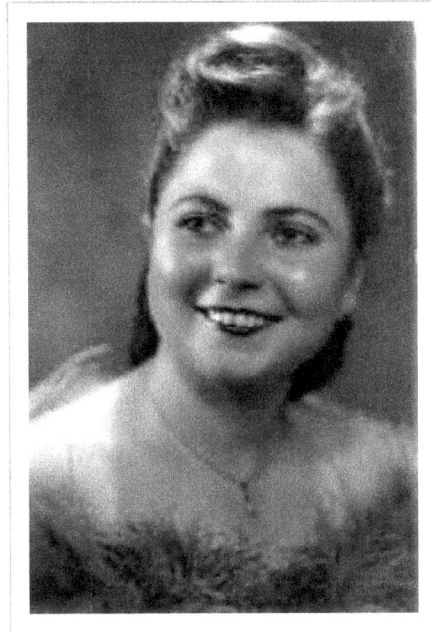

**Masha was a teacher at the Zabzre orphanage**

Seated from left to right: **Dawid Hubel, headmaster; Dr. Nechema Geller, director of the Zabrze orphanage; Captain and later Major Yeshayahu Drucker dressed in his military officer uniform**
Standing left to right: **1 Unknown; 2 Masha; 3 Rudolf Wittenberg, gym teacher and security officer; Mrs. Olnicka; Mrs, Englard, a teacher**

Drucker and Geller worked very hard to assemble a staff that would understand the needs of children who were raised as non–Jews and then would slowly return them to the fold. The children needed a great deal of attention and affection that they had not received for a long time. Extreme patience was required to handle the children. Some of them had lived in many homes and with different families. They were deeply scarred. These children knew that they were Jewish but most of them disliked Jews and Judaism since their environment had taught them that Jews were bad. The Zabrze home slowly built up their confidence by providing them with security, guidance and sense of direction. Most of the children did not stay too long at the orphanage for they were being prepared to go to Palestine. The Hebrew language was emphasized as was the history of the Jewish people. Arts and crafts were stressed since the children could express themselves and release some of their tensions and pressures. Everything had to be done slowly. Some children continued to attend Catholic mass and wear the cross while sitting at the Friday night table with lit candles. Slowly, the children began to learn Jewish practices and customs. The children were exposed to the city and other places.

**Zabrze children touring the city**

The Association of Jewish religious communities in Poland began to popularize the Zabrze home. Some Polish families could not afford to support the children and brought them to the home. Others established contact and inquired as to whether they can expect some reward for caring for a Jewish child during the war. The Zabrze home recorded these inquiries and forwarded them to Drucker.

———

## Footnotes

1. Drucker Tapes
2. Drucker, Testimony, p.38

# Chapter IX

# Pan Kapitan Continues

**Batia Akselrad in 1946 in
France**

Batia Akselrad was another resident at the Zabrze orphanage. She has graciously written her life story in Hebrew for us. Batia recently passed away.

I, Batia Eisenstein–Akselrad, was born on May 5, 1932, in Krosno, Galicia, Poland. My parents were Bendet Akselrad and Cila (nee Freifeld) Akselrad. I had five older brothers. I was the sheltered baby of the family and their worries about my well being greatly increased with the German occupation of the town. The Jewish economic situation in Krosno went from bad to worse with each day. My parents decided to seek shelter for me with a non–Jewish family named Krukierek. Our family was well acquainted with this family whose sons worked at our sawmill in Krosno. The family responded positively to the inquiries.

My mother packed a suitcase of clothing and I packed a small suitcase of items that were dear to me. I took some notebooks, pencils, coloring pencils and some other knickknacks. One evening, my brother, Shalom, took me to my new family. I cried all the way while my brother talked to me about behaving nicely to the family members and to be obedient and respectful. The separation was very difficult and painful. My brother tried his best at soothing my feelings by stating that the family would always be in touch and visit me at the new home. As to my question about why I had to leave the house, there was no immediate answer. Shalom merely said that the family selected a nice and safe place for me where I would be treated as a member of the family. His words gave me some confidence and I ceased crying. We then entered the new home and I was greeted warmly.

**Bendet Akselrad**

My father, Bendet Akselrad, was head of the Jewish communities of Korczyna and Krosno, Galicia, Poland. He was married to Cila Freifeld and they had five sons and a daughter. My oldest brother was Shmuel who was born in 1909 and married to Klara Rosenberg from Debice. They had a daughter named Irenka, born in 1935. My second brother was Shalom, born in 1911. The third brother, Avraham, was born in 1922. The fourth brother was Yehuda, born in 1924, and the fifth brother was Levy, born in 1930. I, Batia Akselrad, was born May 24, 1932.

I will try to describe the family as far as my memories permit. I was a youngster at the time. The family revolved about my father who was devoted to the community. He was a gentle person who had a great deal of patience and listened to everybody who came to the house with a problem and the Jews of Krosno and Korczyna had many problems, mainly survival problems, in a sea of anti–Semitism.

**Cila Freifeld–Akselrad**

As a child I loved the Jewish holidays of Purim, Passover and Friday nights. My father always brought home dinner guests from the synagogue that joined us at the table and shared our meals. Dinners were always interlaced with conversations and discussions. To this day, people who knew my father praise him for his patience, understanding and assistance in solving problems. These people describe to me in great detail his deeds that were unknown to me. These comments make me feel proud of my parents and family.

They also helped me to better understand my father since the people in question dealt with him personally while I was a mere child on the sidelines. Many influential Polish gentiles visited our home and discussed ways and means to avoid or smooth over, sore spots within the Krosno community among Jews and Christians. The Polish population was very anti–Semitic and the slightest incident could turn into a major riot or a pogrom as often happened in the country. The Jews wanted to avoid confrontations at any cost and merely desired to continue with their life that was very difficult, for they faced discrimination at every step of the way. Even gifted Jewish youth could only dream about positions or jobs in governmental or public offices.

Anti–Semitism was deeply embedded among the Polish population and was even transferred from generation to generation with only minor changes.

Father devoted most of his time to the community and considered this task to be his "raison d'etre" or essence of life. He left his various businesses in Krosno to his older sons while he devoted himself to the needs of the Jewish population. The oldest sons Shmuel and Shalom graduated from the school of commerce and administration and managed the various family businesses. Bendet Akselrad was also a graduate of this school. Schooling was very limited to Jews and some trades or professions were closed to Jewish students and in some instances a few Jewish students were admitted as a token of Jewish presence. Mother also helped my father since she received the people who came to the house while father was not at home. She spoke to the visitors and made notations that were relayed to father on his arrival. My brother and I also had important jobs for we ran to open the door whenever the bell rang. Many of the family discussions revolved around the impending war and my parents and older brothers were very perturbed by the news events of the day. I was terrified and expected the worst, especially when I heard the screeching of Hitler on the radio. I had bad feelings but did not really understand what was happening.

The Polish–German war started in September 1939 and my brother Shalom was immediately drafted at night and I was unable to say goodbye to him. Time passed and we heard nothing from Shalom. Then a Pole came to our house and told the family that my brother was seriously injured in his legs and was treated at a hospital in Stanislawow, Eastern Galicia. Of course, he received a nice reward for the information. Father took Avraham and Yehuda with him and they left the house in the direction of the city where Shalom was supposedly convalescing. He left the community affairs in the hands of Shmuel, his oldest son. They soon arrived to Stanislawow and discovered the hoax. Shalom Akselrad was not in the city. But they did meet many Jews from Krosno who had fled to this area prior to the arrival of the Germans. The Akselrads decided to return home but Soviet forces now occupied Stanislawow as part of the partition of Poland by Germany and the Soviet Union. It took some doing and they managed to reach Krosno. Here a postal card awaited him from his son Shalom who was a prisoner of war in a German camp. Shalom continued to send post cards and in one of them he informed us that he would soon be sent home. Our joy was boundless. Father was very busy with the community and was assisted by his elder sons. The city of Krosno had received many Jewish refugees from many places who needed help and temporary lodgings. The Jewish economic situation in the city was very bad, for many Jewish businesses were confiscated and Jews were not permitted to circulate freely in the city. The situation worsened with each day; a white armband with a Star of David had to be worn, anti–Jewish rules and new regulations appeared daily. The situation assumed alarming proportions and my father and brothers barely coped with the situation. They tried to help with whatever they could and the Jews needed all the help that they could get. The fact that father and my brothers spoke German fluently – since the family had lived for many years in Vienna and had Austrian citizenship – gave them the ability to use the language to help the Jews of Krosno.

The Germans refused to deal with Jews and especially those who did not speak German. Every demand had to be written and submitted to the Germans in their language. The Akselrads were busy drafting and writing all kinds of requests for the Jews of Krosno. They also had to follow up these requests and I saw my father's face when he returned with a negative answer. Although I was small, I began to hear strange and meaningless but frightening words like concentration camps, ghetto, searches and Gestapo. I did not understand these words but feared them for they were uttered in fright. I began to mature rapidly as children do in such special circumstances.

One evening father came home and I saw the sadness in his eyes. Mother told me that they wanted to talk to me privately. Father told me that he had found a special place for me with a fine Polish family that wanted to take me to their house. He told me that they would like me very much. I listened seriously but did not really understand what was taking place. Mother packed a bag with clothing. The next evening, my brother Shalom took me to the Krukierek family. During the walk he explained to me how to behave in the new home and to be a good and obedient girl. He instructed me to listen and fulfill all the commands of the new family. He also told me that I now have a new name that I must use. Furthermore, he said, you must not cry or ask to return home. We shall visit you when we can. Parting was very sad; I saw the tears in my brother's eyes and I barely restrained myself from crying. Still, we parted sadly and I entered the new home.

I saw a grandmother, a grandfather and a young couple. Of course, I was very sad since I was left alone when my brother left. The new family named me Basia (a typical

Polish Christian name), as opposed to my name Batia. I cried the entire first night and was unable to fall asleep. I had a hard time adjusting to the idea that I was left alone with a new and strange family. No longer would I be able to rejoin my dear and beloved family. I rose early in the morning and went to the yard. I approached the gate and looked at the path that we used the previous night, but nobody was in sight.

I stood there and cried, hoping to see a familiar face, but no one appeared. I continued to stand or sit there for hours each day in the hope of seeing someone from the family, but in vain. I was depressed and entered the home only when grandfather called me to eat but I had no appetite. Grandmother understood the situation and tried to alleviate my fears by saying that my old family would probably visit me during the day or tomorrow. This of course did not alleviate my depressed feelings but it showed me that someone cared. Needless to say, I was very happy when a member of the family visited and brought a gift from the old home. They always promised to visit me as often as they could to cheer me up, for they saw my red and swollen eyes. They tried to visit often and indeed everybody visited me except my brother Awraham. He went to buy bread and disappeared. The visits always ended in sadness, for I was left alone with my depressed feelings.

My parents and my brothers occasionally visited me except for Avraham. The family visits continued and then suddenly they stopped. My mother Cila Akselrad was caught and shot in 1943 in Korczyna. My father Bendet Akselrad was shot on July 15, 1943, in the concentration camp of Szebnie. My brother Shmuel, his wife Clara, their daughter Irenka, and Shalom Akselrad were caught in Warsaw with false Aryan papers and killed. Avraham Akselrad survived the concentration camps and managed to reach New York where he passed away in 1991 after a lengthy illness. He never established a family. My brother Yehuda Akselrad joined the partisans and fought with them until 1943 when he was killed in the vicinity of Warsaw. My brother Levi was killed in Krosno in 1943. Thus, I was the sole survivor of the family in Krosno and lived with the Polish family.

I missed my parents and brothers and kept dreaming about them. I saw them almost every night in my dreams and was very happy, only to awaken to the bitter reality that I was alone. I was very sad since I wanted the dream to continue, but to no avail. I remained in the house with grandfather and grandmother while the couple went to work. I helped in the house with everything that I could since I tried to please everybody in the family. I was always afraid that I might be kicked out of the house. This fear lingered on and frequently prevented me from sleeping. I slowly became attached to the new family and became more familiar with them. They worried about me and were constantly fearful that an informer might reveal my existence to the Germans. The home of the new family was located in a rural area in the vicinity of the airport of Krosno. Still there was fear that someone might spot this young girl in the courtyard. The Krukierek family decided that the risks of being exposed were serious and took the necessary steps. They began to shift my hiding places. Sometimes I slept hidden in a straw bed in the attic. Others times I was hidden in dark places that affected my vision on seeing light.

On nice evenings, I would emerge and play a bit in the wheat field. Some evenings, grandmother would give me a basket and send me to pick potatoes. I dug the potatoes by hand in the dark so that no one would see me. I picked the big ones and left the small ones in the ground so that they would continue to grow, as grandmother Veronika instructed me to do. I would return with a basket full of potatoes and then clean them before entering the kitchen. Grandfather was pleased with the work and would always say that I earned my keep for the day and would give me an extra heavy slice of bread. I was very proud of my achievements and accepted wholeheartedly these compliments.

Grandfather was rather economical with his compliments; thus I relished them when I received one. Potatoes and cabbage was the standard food of the day for the family. Sunday was a special menu that consisted of potatoes, cabbage and rabbit meat. The latter were raised on the farm next to the cows and roosters. At night I picked potatoes and during the day I tended to the daily house chores. I always volunteered to do extra chores in order to ingratiate myself with the family. The fear of being rejected was always on my mind. I spent a great deal of time peeling potatoes and when I did a good job, I received a slice of bread. I did all the chores with devotion for I craved attention. I wanted to be accepted. Thus, I was very busy in the house, for grandfather had a leg injury and limped, while grandmother was weak and tired easily.

In addition to the regular house chores, I also mended clothing, helped prepare the feed for the cows and did many other kinds of work in the house. Of course, there was less work during the winter when the fields were covered with snow and I spent my time in hiding in the cowshed. The weather was freezing. I spent my time talking to the rabbits and roosters. It seemed to me that they answered but I was not sure if I heard them. I was very lonely and continued to talk to the small animals for I had no friends.

This was a difficult period, for the Germans increased the intensity of their searches and my adopted family was seriously frightened by the new policy. They even considered throwing me out of the place. I was terrified and could not fall asleep for fear of winding up in the street. Grandmother cared a great deal for me and stated that she would assume full responsibility for my protection. Furthermore, she stated that she would leave the house if I were thrown out. Grandmother's threats worked and she saved me. She asked her son Kazek to hide me at the mill where he was a guard. The sawmill belonged to our family prior to the war but was now owned by a German named Schmidt, and Kazek watched the place. He built a hiding place and one night took me from the house in a bag of sawdust.

The hiding place was under a wooden floor amid sawdust. Kazek's brothers also worked at the mill. They had all married and left the household. Only grandmother, grandfather, their married daughter, Jozefa, and myself lived in the house that was near the sawmill. Kazek brought me to the hiding place and gave me instructions on how to behave during the day when the Polish workers tended to their jobs. He also showed me how to position myself in the hiding place so as not to arouse suspicions. I could not sit, move or turn in the dark hiding place. During the day it was still bearable but at night it was frightening. I kept dreaming about my parents and brothers. I had the premonition that they were all killed. I did not want to dream but could not help myself. The dreams continued and I always awakened to stark reality. Furthermore, rats occasionally walked over my body and I could not do a thing about it for there was no room for my hands to move. I was left with the terrible feeling of the creatures walking about me.

For several months I continued to sleep in sawdust under the wooden floor. Autumn was approaching and with it came the rains. Everything was wet and dreary. The cold weather became a reality. Still I had to stay in hiding during the day for fear of being spotted by a worker or by a customer who came to buy wood. Only at night could I slowly venture out As a result of my hiding position, I could barely walk. I was depressed and the thought of ending my life frequently crossed my mind but I was a coward. I did not divulge these thoughts to Kazek for fear of embarrassing him after all his efforts on my behalf.

Winter approached and the family decided to return me to the house. They still hid me here and there but within the house for it was bitter cold outside. I also became accustomed to my new Christian family and realized then that I would never return to Judaism. I no longer wanted to belong to the persecuted and humiliated Jewish people. Grandfather always told me that the Jewish people had always been persecuted throughout history. Even the Arabs were killing the Jews in Palestine. I heard and saw all these things. I saw how Jews were being persecuted while the Christian children played and had fun. I felt jealous and felt ashamed at having been born a Jew.

These thoughts persisted and became stronger as time passed. Suddenly, the roar of shells shook the entire area for we were near the Krosno airport. The Russians shelled the entire area prior to their advance and for several days the cannon fire could be heard and then silence. The area was liberated but nobody came to take me home. I started school for the first time in 1945 and was registered as a Christian student. I excelled in my studies since I devoted myself wholeheartedly to schoolwork. I was a very good student and easily made friends. I felt a certain compensation for all the years spent in terrible deprivation. I also decided to convert to Catholicism; the deed pleased the family and gave me further security at home.

I went to the priest in Krosno and asked to be baptized. He was very surprised and told me that he knew my father. He asked whether there were any survivors in the family and I replied that I was the sole survivor. The priest baptized me on September 5, 1945, and the same month I started school for the first time. I was admitted to the seventh grade in the elementary school for which I was prepared by a private teacher since I had to make up a great deal of schooling. I was a very diligent student and loved to go to school and to study. I made many friends and wanted to be accepted. I tried to make up for all the lost time that I was locked up. I finished elementary school and received a certificate. I was registered to continue schooling the next year and meanwhile I enjoyed the summer recess during which time I met my friends and took trips with them.

My brother Avraham Akselrad survived the camps and slowly recovered from his poor medical condition. He returned to Krosno and came to the Krukierek family to look for me. Avraham Akselrad tried to take me away from the Christian family but saw that he was getting nowhere and he was too weak to fight. He spoke to me about traveling to the Jewish orphanage in Zabrze but I refused. I was determined to stay with the family. I even refused to talk to him. I left the house and hid in the bushes until I was certain that he had left the house. Then I returned home and was furious at my brother for trying to separate me from my new family. He decided to seek legal redress. He contacted the office of Rabbi Kahana and pleaded for help. Yeshayahu Drucker was assigned to the case. Drucker took the case to court since I was a minor. The court heard the case and forced me to stay with my brother at the orphanage in Zabrze for a period of two weeks. The family presented a huge bill of expenses for my upkeep during the war years. The bill had to be paid to the court as a deposit in case I did not return to the family. My brother did not have the necessary cash but he assigned his share of the family property to he Krukierek family if I did not return to their house. My share was untouched since I as a minor. Then the court began to implement the decision. The orphanage was at Zabrze and I was very homesick and wrote letters to the adoptive family but never received a reply. They also wrote letters to me but I did not receive them. The orphanage knew that my adoptive Polish family could kidnap bring me back to their family. The Zabrze home stopped all my correspondence. Shortly thereafter, I was sent to France with a transport of Polish Jewish children.

**Batia Akselrad amongst Polish Jewish children leaving Poland for France**

I remained in Perigueux, France, for two years and then I went to Israel in 1948. I was sent to the agricultural school "Mikveh Israel" and in 1950 I joined the army. In 1953, I married and raised a family. I have two sons and four grandchildren. I live in a private home at Kiriat Ono and tend to my garden. I spend my time attending lectures and reading books.

I continued to write to the Krukierek family and even maintain correspondence with the grandchildren and great grandchildren of the family. Jozefa Krukierek, the woman who kept me hidden during the war years, died in 2002 at the age of 92. I helped her with whatever I could. I continue to correspond with the younger members of the family who do not even know me. But it is important for me to maintain contact with my past.

Signed Batia Eisenstein nee Akselrod

## Michal Heffer

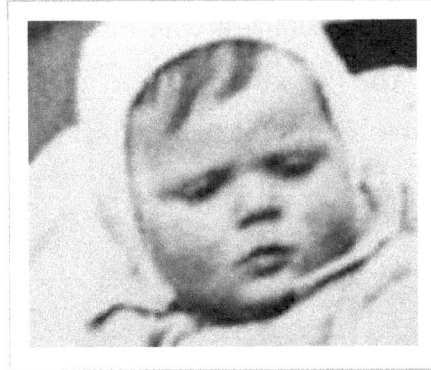

**Michal Heffer (Hinda Zurkowska)
as an infant**

Michal Heffer, formerly Hinda Zurkowska, was another child redeemed by Captain Yeshayahu Drucker. Michal Heffer's family was well established and included many rabbis. Michal was the only member of her family who survived the Nazis. She was smuggled out from the Warsaw Ghetto and handed to a non–Jewish family who in turn handed her over to another family and eventually she wound up in a church nearly 200 kilometers from Warsaw. She was taken in by the local priest, given chores and for a year became a farmhand, tending to the cows and helping out around the church, even singing in the church choir. One day, returning from the fields with the cows, she saw a crowd gathered in front of the church. A big official Polish military car was there and everyone was staring at it. The priest rushed her into the church where she was confronted by a tall, blond Polish military officer and an American in a U.S. Army uniform. She remembers that "The American smiled at me and spoke to me in Polish, reaching into his pocket and showing me photographs of my family, my grandfather, whose picture I imagined I'd seen on the church wall, my mother and others of the family. He said he was my cousin Yehuda Elberg. Then I remembered him; I used to sit on his knee in Warsaw. He'd moved to the U.S. a few years before the war started." At the time Elberg, a journalist, was attached to the U.S. Army's press corps. "The Polish officer produced papers from the court saying that cousin Elberg was my legal guardian," Michal added. "The priest was a little afraid of the Polish officer and the official paper and didn't argue. I gathered up my few things, and got in the big army car. The Polish officer was Yeshayahu Drucker. As was his custom, Drucker left money with the priest for caring for me and risking his life in the process.

We left the house. The village people stared after us. The drive was pleasant but tense in the military car. I was sad on leaving the place where I had spent so much time and became so attached to. I wondered where I was heading and what the future held in store for me. Then, suddenly, the car stopped at a roadblock outside Pilczica, not far from Kielce. We were all forced at gunpoint to step out of the car."

**Michal Heffer with her father and brother prior to World War II**

**Michal Heffer's mother**

The men with weapons were part of the anti–Communist "Armija Krajowa" (home army), the largest para–military underground organization in Poland during the war. The group was extremely nationalistic and anti–Semitic. Jews who joined with them during the war hid their Jewish identity. When the war ended, the Army Krajowa did not stop its para–military activities but continued to harass both the Polish government and any Jewish survivors it came across. This militia considered the communists the enemy of Poland, and the Jews part of the communist plan to take over the country.

**Batia Akselrod Eisenstein (left) Michal Heffer (right) at Zabrze**

Anti–Semitism was rampant in the region around Kielce and Jews were not safe on the roads. Yeshayahu Drucker, in a Polish Army uniform, was in double jeopardy. First, he was part of the Polish army that was an arm of the communist–run government. Second, he was a Jew.

A militia soldier approached Drucker and in a friendly tone asked who he was and why he had a little girl in a Polish military vehicle. Michal Heffer said Drucker then made a nearly fatal mistake. "She's a Jewish girl, we're taking her back to Warsaw," Drucker answered. The militia soldier went back to the commander, who was still at the roadblock, and conferred with him. The soldier came back, pushed Drucker to the side, pulled back the breach of his rifle and was ready to take aim. Drucker realized he was in serious trouble and started talking fast. "You see that guy over there? He's an American officer. A journalist. You shoot me; he'll have it in every newspaper in

America. So you'll have to shoot him, too. You ready to do that?" Confused, the soldier went back to the commander. Another conference ensued. Then the soldier returned, jerked his rifle in the direction of the car. Michal said she and Drucker and Elberg got in, and drove away, fast.

"I thought I was going home with Elberg, but he explained that he couldn't take care of me. Rather I was going to Zabrze, to the Jewish orphanage. And that's where I went with Uncle Elberg and Pan Kapitan."

Drucker visited her at Zabzre, stopping by to say hello when he'd drop off another child, or just come out on a Sunday. According to Michal, many of the children at the Zabrze home considered themselves Christians and even attended church services on Sundays. Pan Kapitan had a great deal of patience with the children and gave them a great deal of attention.

**Michal Heffer**

What is clear from the Heffer story is that in nearly every case, removing Jewish children from non–Jewish homes was a very tedious, delicate and dangerous situation.

Michal went with the second children's transport from Zabrze, Poland, to France where she remained for about two years at Perigueux, France, and then arrived in Israel. She served in the army and they married and raised a family. She lives at her Kfar Vitkin home. Michal is a published author and recognized artist in Israel. She received an award from the state.

**Israeli President Ezer Weitzman awards prize to Michal Heffer**

## Chapter X

# Competition Amongst the Children Homes

Drucker was very busy traveling all over Poland to locate Jewish children in non-Jewish homes. Yeshayahu Drucker not only spoke Polish fluently but looked Polish. This would be a very important attribute because, when Drucker presented himself at the home of a Polish farmer and talked about a Jewish child who lived with the family, the farmer assumed that the Polish government wanted the matter settled. Drucker had lists and addresses of Jewish children in non-Jewish homes. His job was to travel around Poland and locate the hidden Jewish children. Then the process of negotiations started. Sometimes he had names and addresses from letters supplied by Rabbi Kahana or Rabbi Herzog or other Jewish sources or testimonies in which surviving Jews provided information about the location of Jewish children in non-Jewish homes. Drucker would arrive in his uniform in a military car driven by a military chauffer, supplied by Rabbi Kahane.[1] No Polish farmer could believe that he faced a Jew.

The fact that Drucker approached the holders of the Jewish children with money incentives and praise for their action during the war placed the negotiations on a friendly basis and contributed to the high degree of Drucker's success. At first his approaches were usually rejected, but he would stubbornly persist. He would visit frequently, bringing candy and toys for the children and gifts for the family. Slowly he would begin to negotiate with the Polish families or Christian institutions and pay the families or institutions for their financial outlay during the war. Occasionally, if a family did not negotiate honestly or worse, flatly refused to negotiate, he used guile and even force to bring the Jewish children from their Christian homes. Although he sometimes used forceful methods to get the child, he always managed to pay for the child's upkeep during the war. The redemption campaign of the Jewish religious association proved to be very popular with the surviving Jews in Poland who finally found someone who actively helped them in their struggle to recover surviving members of their family.

These successful activities created resentments at the Jewish education department of the Central Committee of Polish Jews. As we already mentioned, the committee had the full backing of the Polish government in Warsaw. The central committee's education department, under the leadership of Shlomo Herszenhorn, ran most of the Jewish orphanages in postwar Poland. Herszenhorn was an important Bund leader, a member of the central committee and headed the education programs of Jewish education. His department had the largest number of Jewish orphanages in postwar Poland. His first children's home was opened in Lublin in July, 1944 with that city's liberation. Following the end of the war, this organization immediately proceeded to set up homes for the surviving Jewish orphans. Rabbi Kahana did not like the content of the educational programs at the homes. He was interested in the restoration of Jewish religious life in Poland. The Polish government refused to involve itself in a fight between the central committee and the Jewish religious associations headed by Rabbi Kahane. The Polish government did not want to antagonize Jewish organizations throughout the world. It wanted to show a fair attitude to the Jews in Poland in its fight with the reactionary policies of the Polish government in exile in London. So the central committee was told to keep away from the religious associations. The central committee had to accept the decision.

The central committee did not concern itself with Jewish children in non–Jewish homes unless they were mistreated. The Jewish religious associations, that is, Drucker, actively searched for Jewish children hidden in Christian homes and institutions. On occasion, relatives of the children at the homes of the central committee induced the children to leave these homes and Zionist homes or Zionist religious homes where they received a Zionist education. These acts irritated the central committee that constantly shifted to the political left. Soon another threat and a more dangerous threat appeared.

The Zionist parties in Poland began to emerge and began to create Jewish institutions, orphanages and kibbutzim for older youngsters. Most of them were impressed by the activities of the Jewish religious associations in Poland. Soon there was tremendous competition among the various Zionist organizations in retrieving Jewish children from Christian places. The fight became intensive and acrimonious with the arrival of large numbers of repatriated Jewish orphans from Russia. The various Zionist homes began to entice youngsters to leave their current Zionist homes and join other Zionist homes. The competition among the various Jewish organizations greatly increased the price of redemption of Jewish children. Some people even demanded cash in dollars for the release of Jewish children, Of course, the homes of the central Jewish committee were also affected by the enticements and desertions of Jewish children but they could do little since the Polish government did not want to interfere. Then, Arieh Sharid, an emissary from Palestine, suggested that all the Zionist parties form a head office called "The Zionist Coordination Office" under the leadership of Leibel Korinski from Kibbutz Yagur in Palestine. He coordinated the activities of redeeming Jewish children. The office established four homes where youngsters remained for some time until they left Poland. The office also began to establish and coordinate various Zionist orphanages for Jewish orphans who returned from Russia.

Most of the Zionist organizations that belonged to this office were non–religious and their orphanage homes followed a secular Zionist base of instruction. Rabbi Kahana and Rabbi Becker helped to establish religious Zionist homes under the auspices of the Mizrahi and Hapoel Hamizrahi political movements. Similar homes were established by the non–Zionist Orthodox Agudat Israel party. The religious parties were not part of the "Koordinacja" central committee. The aim of the office and the Zionist homes was to prepare the children to head for Palestine. Indeed, transports of children constantly left Poland, some legally as was the case of the large Herzog children's transport that will be described below. Other large transports of children went to Britain with Rabbi Solomon Schonfeld and some children headed to the DP camps in Germany and Austria. Many Jewish children left Poland illegally by various means. Some children were officially adopted by Jewish families abroad. The Polish government was aware of the situation but refused to stop these illegal activities for fear of tarnishing further its bad reputation regarding Jews in Poland.

The Zabrze home and the Gluszyca home were not affiliated with the Zionist Coordination office or the Zionist organizations or with the Central Committee homes that were the largest in number. Both homes belonged to the Association of Religious Jewish communities in Poland. The head of the association was Rabbi Kahana, a military chaplain; his assistants were Captain Yeshayahu Drucker, and Captain Rabbi

Becker. Essentially the organization was under the auspices of the Polish army, which paid their salaries. Both homes prepared the children for Jewish life and intended to ship them to Palestine. It is estimated that 600–700 children stayed at the Zabrze home for various periods of time until they left Poland. The homes devoted themselves to the children and to their needs, which were extensive. The children demanded constant attention and particularly individual attention, which they never received in their previous places. They acted out their fears, imagined or real, and the staff had to help and offer guidance to the youngsters. The homes used a great deal of social psychology in drawing out the children from their isolation by involving them in big plays that involved many children. According to David Danieli, the Zabzre home staged celebrations on the birthdays of Theodor Herzl, the founder and leader of political Zionism, and Chaim Nachman Bialik, the great modern Hebrew writer.

Meanwhile large transports of Polish refuges arrived from the Soviet Union. These transports contained a substantial number of Jews and many Jewish orphans in the Polish orphanages. Technically speaking these children were supposed to go to the homes of the Central Committee. Rabbi Kahana and Drucker were bitterly opposed to these homes. They awaited transport trains and talked the Jewish children to leave the Polish or Central orphanages. The older Jewish children were very happy to leave the Polish institutions where they were mistreated. The chaplains and the Jewish religious communities in Poland tried to find temporary homes for these children. Rabbi Kahana and the chaplains decided to look for a home for these children. A place was soon located near the city of Walbrzych named Gluszyca. Several hundred repatriated Polish Jews settled in this hamlet. The house was soon provided with all the necessary facilities and Jewish youths soon moved in. A section of the home was reserved for elderly Jews. The children were older than the Zabrze children and most of them did not speak Polish. Some Jewish parents brought their children to the Gluszyca home since they could not provide for them. The atmosphere was more religious at the home. The home stressed Hebrew, Palestine geography and Zionism.

The Jewish religious communities in Poland helped many youngsters to reach the Gluszyca home. Rabbi Aaron Becker devoted himself more to Gluszyca while Rabbi Yeshayahu Drucker devoted himself to Zabrze. Both chaplains fought for each Jewish child. The competition for Jewish children increased with time as many Zionist organizations and non–Zionist organizations began to open homes for Jewish orphans.

Frequently there were scenes at the railroad stations between the various organizations trying to get some Jewish orphans to join their homes. The Central Committee did not involve itself in these activities but lost many children to the other Jewish homes that stressed Jewish values.

**The Gluszyca home for children and old people, 1946–1947**

**Chanukah lighting ceremony at Gluszyca orphanage**

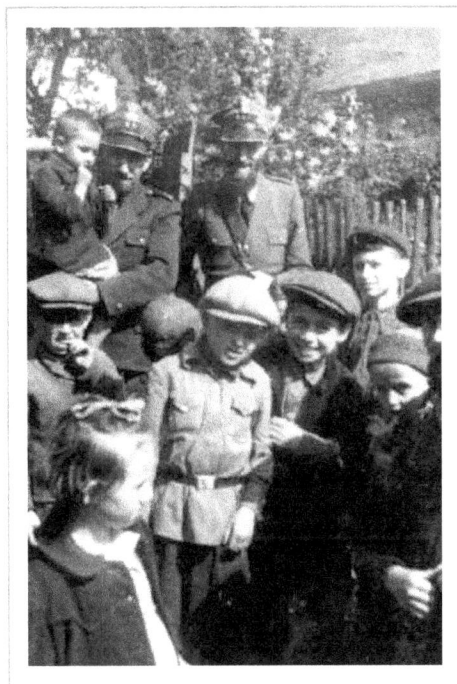

**Rabbi Kahana and Rabbi Becker at the Gluszyca home**

**Rabbi Kahana adrressed the orphans at Gluszyca home**

The Gluszyca home would operate from about 1946 to 1947. With the end of the mass transports from the Soviet Union the number of Jewish children declined and the home closed. Most of the children were sent out of Poland by various means. Zabrze continued to operate and even received some publicity amongst the non-Jewish population. The orphanages began to work and received children from Christian families that surrendered the children and were compensated for their expenses of caring for the Jewish children during the war.

Zabrze was always in need of money for the expenses of redeeming Jewish children and running the home was very expensive. Contributions came from various places and institutions throughout the Jewish world, as the one below.

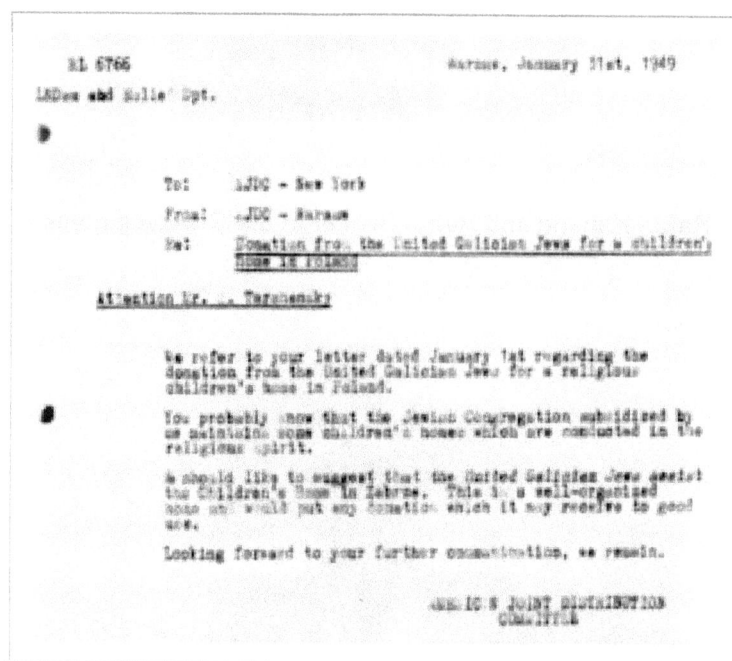

**Contribution made by the Association of the United Galician Jews to the Zabrze home via the JDC organization in Poland**

These donations kept flowing to Poland and helped the Association of Jewish religious communities and the Jewish religious homes to provide the needed services to the Jewish communities. The fact that Rabbi Kahana was the chief chaplain of the Polish army established him as the leader of Polish religious Jewry. His office became the center of information regarding Jewish religious and non–religious matters in Poland. Rabbis wrote letters to him and frequently sent contributions or gifts to his office so that he could provide the restored Jewish communities with prayer books or bibles or prayer shawls. Drucker, of course, saw to it that the Zabrze home received all the religious items that the children needed.

The biggest and largest contributor to the maintenance of the home was of course the Polish JDC headed by David Guzik, director of the Joint Distribution Committee's operations in Poland.

David Guzik was born in Warsaw, Poland. He joined the JDC Warsaw office as an accountant in 1918. During the course of World War II, he became a central figure in JDC Warsaw. Using his skills to raise funds by legal or illegal means, he helped finance welfare services, medical help, and cultural and underground activities in the ghetto including the Oneg Shabbat project and the Warsaw Ghetto Uprising. He survived the war in hiding on the "Aryan" side. In 1945, he was appointed Director of JDC Operations in liberated Poland. David Guzik was killed in a plane crash in Prague in 1946 while returning from a conference in Paris, France. He had gone to Paris for consultations and met Joseph Schwartz, head of JDC operations in Europe. The tragic loss of Guzik at this period was a great loss to the JDC in Poland. The place needed someone that was familiar with the country and with problems that the surviving Shoah Jews faced. Schwartz decided to call on William Beim who was JDC director in Poland between the wars. Beim answered the call and returned to Poland.

**David Guzik**

Dr. Joseph Schwartz was a brilliant and exceptional man. Known as Packy to those close to him, he was born in Ukraine and moved to Baltimore at an early age. A distinguished educator and scholar and an authority on Semitics and Semitic Literature, Dr. Schwartz received his doctorate from Yale, following his graduation from the Rabbi Isaac Elchanan Seminary of Yeshiva University. Dr. Schwartz taught at the American University in Cairo and at Long Island University and then served as Director of the Federation of Jewish Charities in Brooklyn. He served the JDC from 1939–1950, and then went on to become the Executive Vice Chairman of the United Jewish Appeal and later the Vice President of Israel Bonds. He passed away in 1975, leaving behind a legacy of countless good deeds.

Following World War II, Dr. Schwartz organized a massive organization that helped thousands of Shoah survivors and enabled them to regain their humanity. The Joint Distribution Committee not only provided food, medicine and financial help but also provided hope. Schwartz was especially concerned with the Jewish infants who had survived the war. Orphanages and Jewish youth centers were on top of his list. He, of course, endorsed the support for the Zabrze orphanage.

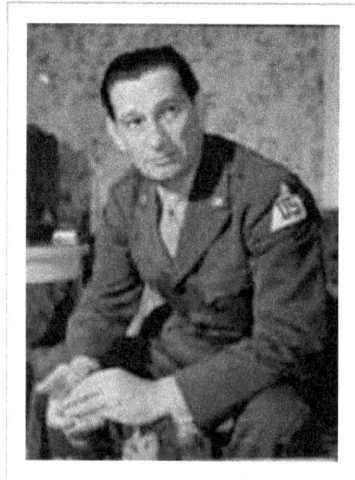

**Dr. Joseph Schwartz in his
military uniform**

## Partial JDC Archives List of Children's Homes in Poland
Notice Zabrze is listed as a religious congregation.

| Institution | Address | Number of children |
|---|---|---|
| TOZ, Jewish Health Assc | Otwock, Olin | 40 Sanatorium |
| | Glussyoe | 80 Preventorium |
| | Srodborow Cleszynska | 70 |
| Religious Organizations Agudas Israel | Krakow Dreitele | 29 |
| | Dzierszew | 50 |
| | Lodz | 10 |
| Children Home | Dzierzoniow, Browarna12 | 30 |
| | Lodz, Zachodnia 66 | 10 |
| Religious Congregation | Zabrze, Karlowicza 10 | 31 |
| Vaad Hatzala | Bytom, Smolenska 15 | 70 |
| Zionist Organizations | Headquarters, Lodz | |
| | Poludniowa | 26 |
| Mizrachi | Krakow, Miodova 26 | 25 |
| Mizrachi | Sosnowiec | 39 |
| Coordination of Zionist | Lodz, Zawadzka 17 | 93 |
| Hashomer Hazair | Srodmiejska 4 | 49 |
| Poale Zion | Bielawa | 52 |
| Central Jewish home | Committee Legnica, Piastowska 6 | 60 |
| Central Jewish home | Piotrolesie, Ogrodowa 10 | 88 |
| Central Jewish home | Chorsow, Katowicka 2 | 80 |
| Central Jewish home | Otwock, Bolesl. Pruss 11 | 80 |
| Central Jewish home | Srodborow, Cieszynska | 75 |
| Central Jewish home | Bielsko, Mickiewicza 22 | 56 |
| Central Jewish home | Srodborow, Literacka 2 | |
| Central Jewish home | Srodborowianka" | 104 |
| Central Jewish home | Helenowek | 117 |
| Central Jewish home | Krakow, Augustyuska Boczna 8 | 66 |

The original list is very difficult to read so we transcribed it for the readers.

The first column on the left gives the name of the organization of the home. The word central indicates that the home was under the control of the Central Committee of Polish Jews. The second column gives the address of the home and the last column indicates the number of children at the time of the visit of the inspectors of the Joint Distribution Committee. The number of children in the central homes remained relatively steady while the Zionist or Agudah homes constantly changed since the children were constantly shipped out of Poland.

The insecurity of the Jewish population in Poland was also felt at the Jewish orphanages. The Zabrze home took several defensive measures, namely the entrance doors were constantly closed and watched especially at night. Danieli was even sent to the place where he lived to dig up several "Mauser" hand guns that he handed to Rudolf Wittenberg to use them to defend the Zabrze compound. The "Ichud" kibbutz that happened to be at the Zabrze Jewish compound was charged with the defense of the home. We already mentioned that The Ichud organization maintained a training farm within the Jewish compound of Zabrze. Apparently, they assumed the defense of the place. Of course, this was a temporary measure, most homes wanted to send their children out of Poland except for the homes under the control of the Central Committee of Polish Jews. These homes tried to educate the Jewish youngsters in a theoretical view of Polish spirit that did not exist. Even the children saw that they were being attacked because they were Jewish. Many of these children left these homes and joined Zionist homes or kibbutzim in order to get out of Poland.

———————

## Footnote

1.   Drucker testimony at Yad Vashem

Chapter XI

# Yeshayahu Drucker Gives Everything to the Home

According to Noah –Libes formerly Anna Druker mentioned earlier, Zabrze was a nice and comfortable home[1]. Most of the children were girls, for it was more difficult to protect Jewish boys who were circumcised. Most of the children were orphans or half orphans namely they had one parent. The atmosphere at the home was relaxed and easy going. The director and the staff created a pleasant environment that encouraged the orphans to feel at

**Staff and children at Zabrze celebrate the festival of Lag B'Omer**

At ease in spite of their past experiences. The orphanage stressed living together within the compound and avoided contact with the outside Polish population. Most of the children had little or no contact with Judaism that was slowly spoon fed to the children. Yeshayahu Drucker, nicknamed Pan Kapitan by the children, devoted much time and energy to tell Jewish stories to the children. The staff was encouraged to stage plays connected with Jewish events or holidays. Members of the staff related to the children with a great deal of patience and understanding. Nobody spoke to the children about their experiences, pains and traumatic experiences. Judaism was slowly introduced by the staff especially by Pan Kapitan following the Friday night meals when all the children were dressed in their best. At the sight of the Shabbat candles Pan Kapitan slowly told stories that dealt with Jewish figures. The children were fascinated by these stories that glorified the Jews. He was adored by the children and Noah felt proud of being related to her so called uncle. He was very pleased that she stopped her Christian daily prayers with her arrival to Zabrze. She did not accept Judaism but neither practiced Christianity.

**Zabrze staff and children celebrate Herzl's birthday**
Notice Pan Kapitan in military uniform holding a child

**Zabrze children perform group dances**

**Memorializing the Warsaw Jewish Ghetto uprising**

The food was excellent at the home. The children received very nice American clothes at the home. In short, life was good. Then, one day there was a celebration when the State of Israel was proclaimed. The children sang the songs that were taught at the home by a music teacher. The Zabrze home devoted a great deal of time to plays, ceremonies, and festive presentations that emphasized Jewish history and tradition, yet another way to inculcate Jewish values to the children who had been deprived of their heritage.

Many children were involved in these presentations or in the preparations of the shows. Children constantly arrived at Zabrze or left Zabrze. Priority was of course given to children who had relatives and wanted them. Some of the children remained at Zabrze for a short period of time until papers were obtained. The Polish government followed a liberal policy regarding surviving orphans joining their families. Small children presented a special problem since they needed a great deal attention and care that Zabrze could not provide. Rabbi Salomon Schonfeld, son in law of the chief rabbi of England rabbi Joseph Hertz, organized two transports of small children that were sent directly to England from Poland.

Rabbi Schonfeld was an experienced hand in rescuing Jewish children from Europe before World War II. He was very active in bringing children from Germany and Austria and placing them with religious Jewish families. Eventually the families adopted the children. With the end of the war he immersed himself in rescuing Jewish children from non–Jewish homes. He worked very closely with Rabbi Kahana and mostly with Drucker. Rabbi Schonfeld helped the Jewish homes financially and materially. Rabbi Schonfeld made all the arrangements in England to bring small Jewish children and place them with Jewish families. Drucker and Rabbi Kahana helped to get the transports out of Poland. Esther Kastenbaum was one of the young escorts from Zabrze who took a group of small children to England. They left Poland by plane and flew to England where families awaited the transport. The children were assigned to the families in accordance with prearranged plans. The children escorts remained in England where they helped the children get s established. Esther Kastenbaum, one of the escorts, remained with an adopted family for some time since the adopted child experienced difficulties in relating to the new family. After a while, she moved out but continued to visit the family. These visits soon stopped and the child became part of the family. Esther remained in England and continued her education with the help of Rabbi Schonfeld. She became a nurse. Eventually she moved to Israel.

**Rabbi Salomon Schonfeld dressed in military uniform**

**Rabbi Salomon Schonfeld on the left with a group of British couples that adopted Jewish children from Zabzre**

Pan Kapitan was a one-man team. He worked alone and obtained results. He had difficulty working with other organizations that were also interested in rescuing children, namely the Zionist organizations. The latter worked with offices and directives while Pan Kapitan was his own boss. His office was part of the Polish state and he wore the Polish uniform, which opened many doors to him. Pan Kapitan had lists and addresses of Jewish children in non–Jewish homes. His job was to travel around Poland and locate the hidden Jewish children. Then the process of negotiations started. Sometimes he had names and addresses from letters supplied by Rabbi Kahana or Rabbi Herzog or other Jewish sources or testimonies in which surviving Jews provided information about the location of Jewish children in non–Jewish homes.[2]

The fact that Pan Kapitan approached the holders of the Jewish children with money incentives and praise for their action during the war placed the negotiations on a friendly basis and contributed to the high degree of Pan Kapitan's success. At first his approaches were usually rejected, but he would stubbornly persist. He would visit frequently, bringing candy and toys for the children and gifts for the family. Slowly he would begin to negotiate with the Polish families or Christian institutions and pay the families or institutions for their financial outlay during the war. Occasionally, if a family did not negotiate honestly or worse, took money and refused to abide by the agreement, he used guile and even force to bring the Jewish children from the Christian homes. Although he sometimes used forceful methods to get the child, he always managed to pay for the child's upkeep during the war. The redemption campaign of the Jewish religious association proved to be very popular with the surviving Jews in Poland who finally found someone who actively helped them in their struggle to recover surviving members of their family.

Pan Kapitan's successful activities gave him wide publicity throughout the Jewish world. Rabbis and organizations pleaded for help in locating Jewish children. The rabbinate's office in Jerusalem, Palestine received a great deal of mail regarding Jewish children living with non–Jewish families. We already mentioned that that the orphanages of the Central Committee of Polish Jews took no action to remove Jewish children from non–Jewish homes, on occasion they paid monthly allotments to the Polish families or institutions that kept Jewish children. Thus, the affected families turned to the Palestinian rabbinate for help. Rabbi Herzog was swamped with the mail and correspondence. He enlisted the aid of his son Yaacov Herzog with the mail.

**Yaakov David Herzog**

Rabbi Yaacov David Herzog, was a graduate of the elite Hebron Yeshiva in Palestine, an ordained rabbi, and a member of the Haganah, the secret Jewish underground operating in Palestine for the establishment of a Jewish homeland. Yaakov David Herzog was highly competent, personable, and skilled at handling most of the correspondence that crossed his father's desk. Yaacov quickly became indispensable to his father, not only as a bureau chief, but also as an important member of his father's staff. Below is a letter that Yaakov wrote directly to Pan Kapitan in Warsaw. The letter is in Hebrew and attached was a list of names that is illegible.

ו' טבת תש'ז.

לכבוד
ידידנו הנכבד הקפיטן דרוקי,
וארשה.
ר.מ.נ.

הרינו מצרפים לו נזה רסימה
של ילדים הנמצאים בידי נכרים, או מקרים
אהרים בפולין. קרוביהם בארץ מבקשים אלינו
הבקשה להצילם, או לפחות להכניסם לידי
מרתדרונ יהודים רפולין. נביר לו תודה
מודה, אם יואיל לטפל נכל המקרים האלה
ולהודיענו במרוטרוט את התוצאות.

נשמח מאד לעמוד אתו בקשר מתמיד
הדוק.

בכבוד רב
ובברכת התורה והארץ,

יעקב הרצוג.

A loose English translation of the letter dated January 27, 1946.

To our esteemed friend, Captain Drucker
Warsaw
R.M.N.

We attach to the note a list of names of Jewish children who find themselves in a non–Jewish environment in Poland. Their relatives in Palestine asked us to save them or at least place them in Jewish homes in Poland. We are thanking you for all the efforts. We would appreciate if you could check the status of these children and please keep us informed as to the results.

Please keep in touch.

 Yours,

With blessings from the Torah and the Holy Land.

 Yaakov Herzog

בס"ד, חיפה, כ"ט בחשרי ה'תש"ז    דניאל שטראוס וייפה
(24.10.46)    רחוב החרמון מס.33

לכבוד
הרב הראשי לארץ ישראל
מרן הרב הרצוג שליט"א
י ר ו ש ל י ם

רב גדול ושלום,    הנדון: הצלת נפש ופניון שבויים.

הנני מבקש בזה רשות מאת כת"ר לפנות אליו בענין דחוף של פקוח נפש
דלקמן:

לפני זמן מה נודע לי שילדתו של אחי, שהיה דר בפרג שבצ'יכוסלובקיה,
מירי שטראוס, שמלאו לה רק עכטיו 9 שנים, נשארה בחיים והיא נמצאה אצל
משפחה נוצרית בפולין במחוז זמוסק, כפי הפרטים הרשומים מטה.

הואיל וכת"ר שהה אז בחוץ-לארץ, פניתי במפעתו ל"ג'וינט" בירושלים
ובקשתי מהם לברר את הדבר ולהשתדל להציל את הילדה הזו מהידים הנוצריות.
כעת קבלתי מכתב מהג'וינט" (מספר 24124/6/1) בו הם מודיעים לי
שהועד היהודי המקומי בזמוסק הודיע כי הילדה מירי שטראוס נמצאת ערינ'ידי
הנוצרי, והוא מוכן למסור את הילדה תמורה פיצויים בעד ההוצאות שהיו לו בקשר
עם חינוכה בזמן היותה אצלו.

מצד אחד, לא היה קץ לשמחתי לבשורה הטאהרה שהילדה אמנם נמצאה בחיים,
אולם מהצד השני, נגדם לי גם צער רב וחרדה גדולה ע"י הידיעה שהילדה ערינ
נמצאת בידיים זרות ...

אין לי כל רשות וכוונה לבוא לעיגשר בטענות, אולם יחד עם זאת,
כואב לבי מאוד מאוד שהוועד היהודי בזמוסק לא יכול היה למצוא עד היום
את האפשרות להציל את הילדה הרבה מהידים הרבה בצערני הגדרית.

במצב הנוכחי העגוב של היהודים בפולין ובפרט הנני חרד ודואג מאוד מאוד
לגורלה של הילדה, הצדיר היחיד של"ע נמצא לפליטה מכל המשפחה. וכיהוך הנני
חרד בגלל "החינוך" שילדה רכה זו, בת 9 מקשיבה לקבל...

אני יודע שעד כמה שאפשר להקדים לשחרר את הנפש התמימה הזו מהשפעת
התחינוך הנ"ל, הוא חשוב עד מאוד, וכל יום וכל שעה הם יקרים; אך לצערי מאא
העמוק, קצרה ידי מלהושיע ...

הנני מתפרנס מיגיע כפי, ואני יכול להתחייב לפרנס את הילדה ביד
אחרי עלותה ארצה, והיא לא תפול חו"ש בשום אומן למעמסה על הצבור; אולם,
לדאבוני, אין לי כל חכמות כדי להשתתף בתשלום הפיצויים הדרושים.

לכן הנני פונה אל מעלת כת"ר בכל לשון של בקשה שיואיל להשתמש בכל
השפעתו, כדי לזרז את ה"ג'וינט", או אולי כת"ר בעצמו ימצא בע"ה דרך יותר
מהירה כדי להציל את הנפש הרבה הזו מצפרני הזרים, ובעיקר, מהשפעה "החינוך"
שהיא ממשיכה לקבל ...

הנני מאמין שכת"ר ידיעתה כעיטב יכלחו להחיש פעולת הצלה זו, כדי
שילדה רכה זו, בת 9, תוכל להתחיל לקבל חינוך יהודי, ואלוקי ציון יגליה את
ירכו בכל פעולותיו הכבירות למען הנדון השבויים והצלת הנפשות שכח"ל מחסד
להם בכל לבבו ונפשו.

אין בפי די מלים להנצ לכת"ר את רגשי תודתי העמוקה ואלוקי ציון
ישלם לו כערכו.

לידיעה על עזרתו הנניא מצמה בכלירן נפש.

ברגשי כבוד והערצה

דניאל שטראוס

| | | | |
|---|---|---|---|
| הכתובת הנוכחית | | הפרטים על הילדה | |
| GLAGOLA | שם הנוצרי המחזיק בה | Leopold Straus | שם האב |
| BIALOWDLE | שם הכפר | Alice (Steiner) | שם האם |
| Poland המדינה ZAMOS | המחוז | Miri | שם הילדה |
| C.S.R. PRAHA via U. Nezorky | מקום מגורם העודם | | |
| PRAHA C.S.R. | מקום הלידה של הילדה | | |

**Another plea to Rabbi Herzog to intervene on behalf of a Jewish child kept in a non–Jewish home**
Notice the notation on the top of the letter in pen, on the left side, direct the letter to Drucker

Drucker received not only appeal letters from Palestine, the USA, England but also from within Poland. Searching, locating, and removing Jewish children from non-Jewish environment became his main and full time occupation. Weekends he frequently spent with the children at the Zabrze orphanage. Of course, he always tried to bring sweets or goodies to the children. He spent hours talking and listening to the children who nicknamed him Pan Kapitan. The name would remain with him for life.

Soon another threat and a more dangerous threat appeared.

The Zionist parties in Poland began to emerge and began to create Jewish institutions, orphanages and kibbutzim for older youngsters. Most of them were impressed by the activities of the Jewish religious associations in Poland. Soon there was tremendous competition among the various Zionist organizations in retrieving Jewish children from Christian places. The fight became intensive and acrimonious with the arrival of large numbers of repatriated Jewish orphans from Russia. The various Zionist homes began to entice youngsters to leave their current homes, central or Zionist homes and join other Zionist homes. The competition among the various Jewish organizations greatly increased the price of redemption of Jewish children. Some people even demanded cash in dollars for the release of Jewish children. The Zionist organizations decided to establish a united office to redeem Jewish children. The organizations appointed Arieh Sharid formerly Leibele Goldberg, a member of kibbutz Yagur and representative of the Palestinian Labor Movement. He was one of the first emissaries to be sent to Poland where he was born and later left for Palestine as a pioneer. He was instructed to form a united negotiating office to redeem Jewish children from Christian homes. He began negotiations between the various Zionist parties to establish a common front. Long negotiations ensued and finally he managed to establish "The Zionist Coordination Office" under the leadership of Leibel Koriski member of Ha–Shomer Ha–Ttzair. He would run the united office from 1946 to 1948 when he returned to Palestine. Koriski worked under the auspices of a central committee that included almost all political Zionist parties with the exception of the religious and revisionist parties. Even WIZO was included. WIZO stands for " The Women's International Zionist Organization", a volunteer organization dedicated to social welfare in all sectors of Israeli society, the advancement of the status of women, and Jewish education in Israel and the Diaspora. The board coordinated the activities of redeeming Jewish children. The office established four homes where youngsters remained for some time until they left Poland. The office also began to establish and coordinate various Zionist orphanages for Jewish orphans who returned from Russia.

Most of the Zionist organizations that belonged to this office were non–religious and their orphanage homes followed a secular Zionist base of instruction. Rabbi Kahane and Rabbi Becker helped to establish religious Zionist homes under the auspices of the Mizrahi and Hapoel Hamizrahi, political movements orphanages that had been established in Krakow at Miodowa Street and in Sosnowiec. Similar homes were established by the non–Zionist Orthodox Agudat Israel party at Dzierszew. The religious parties were not part of the "Koordinacja" central committee. The aim of the office and the Zionist homes was to prepare the children to head for Palestine. Indeed, transports of children constantly left Poland, some legally as was the case of the large Herzog children's transport or Schonfeld's transports and some children headed illegally to the DP camps in Germany and Austria under the guide of the Brichah organization. Some children were officially adopted by Jewish families abroad. The Polish government was aware of the situation but refused to stop these illegal activities for fear of tarnishing further its bad reputation regarding Jews in Poland.

The situation for Polish Jews went from bad to worse and reached its high point with the Kielce pogrom. The Jews in Kielce were accused of killing a Christian child for the blood needed to bake matzot, the unleavened bread Jews use during the Passover holiday. This "blood–libel" was readily accepted by the Polish masses, who rampaged through the streets, killing any Jews they found in the city. The mob was joined by members of the Polish police and other Polish security forces, even though these forces all had to be members of the Communist Party in order to get and keep their jobs. Exacerbating this situation were the nationalist forces that tried to bring down the government. They pointed to the Jews holding cabinet posts like Yaacov Berman, something unheard of in Poland before World War II, as proof that the Jews control Poland. These Jews were of course members of the Communist party therefore all Jews, especially those that returned from the Soviet Union were all Communists. The Polish masses bought these stories that led to minor anti–Jewish incidents throughout Poland and culminated in the Kielce pogrom where 42 Jewish survivors of the Shoah were killed and about 40 were injured on July 4, 1946[3]. Polish soldiers, and police officers, joined the mob. The government had to rush special-forces to restore order.

The alarm was sounded to the surviving Jews that there was no safety for Jews in Poland. Jews packed their bags and began to leave en masse.

**The burial of the Jewish pogrom victims in Kielce Poland**

The Jewish orphanages also began to expedite the process of removing Jewish youngsters from their homes in Poland. Rabbi Herzog was meeting many influential political figures mainly in Prague, Czechoslovakia to get permission for a transport of Jewish children to enter the country, and remain for a while, until accommodations could be found in France and Belgium. He finally received all permits and headed to Poland where he stayed at the Warszawa Hotel, as the guest of Rabbi Kahana. The two rabbis exchanged ideas and plans. Rabbi Herzog learned more about the Jewish orphanages that had been set up by Rabbi Kahane to house the Jewish children redeemed from Christian homes and institutions.

During the conversation Rabbi Herzog reached the conclusion that the French and Belgian entry permits he'd obtained could now be used. Rabbi Kahana suggested that perhaps the children could join the hoards of Jews already illegally crossing into Czechoslovakia on the way to DP camps in Germany and Italy. Rabbi Herzog felt that the children had suffered enough and were entitled to travel to Paris like human beings. Rabbi Kahana ordered Drucker to meet with all the homes that would be sending children with the transport and instruct them to prepare all the necessary papers so that the departure could be immediate. Drucker asked for lists of would–be travelers so that all travel arrangements could be made. The time had finally come to bring these children out of their tenuous situation to a chance of a decent future.

Rabbi Kahana also arranged for Rabbi Herzog to meet important Polish Jewish leaders, Polish government officials and members of the Polish parliament in order to further his plans for the children's departure. One meeting was between Rabbi Herzog and Poland's Prime Minister Eduard Osobka–Morawski. The meeting was cordial. Rabbi Herzog asked the Polish leader to introduce legislation that all Jewish children residing in Poland be recognized as Jews even if these children no longer lived with Jewish families or in a Jewish environment. Rabbi Herzog also requested the Polish prime minister to allow 750 Jewish orphans and 500 yeshiva students to leave Poland for Palestine. Prime Minister Osobka–Morawski consented to Rabbi Herzog's request. Osobka–Morawski ordered the Polish Red Cross to arrange a train to carry the Jewish children to Paris and bring back to Poland injured and disabled Polish citizens from France. The Polish Red Cross was to prepare all the details with the UNRRA organization. Secrecy was to be maintained so as not to alarm Britain.

Soon, Rabbi Herzog was approached by a committee headed by Mr. R. Berger, chief welfare and repatriation officer of UNRRA, the Polish Red Cross, Polish officials, and Jewish officials, excluding the JDC, but including the American Vaad Hatzala. At the meeting Rabbi Herzog was pleased to learn that UNRRA would absorb the costs of the children's transportation, food and housing. He did try to meet with the Catholic hierarchy in Warsaw, but was not granted an interview. Accompanied by Polish security, that somewhat inhibited his movements the rabbi also had only minimal contact with the Central Jewish Committee of Polish Jews, the group that was overwhelmingly opposed to Palestine, Zionism, religious Judaism and to Jews leaving Poland. Rabbi Herzog was relieved when Rabbi Kahana informed him that the Polish government had provided all the necessary papers for the children's departure. He also learned that the UNRRA transport committee was preparing a document detailing every aspect of the train, Rabbi Herzog organized a press conference in Warsaw and addressed the English and American correspondents in Warsaw, speaking mostly about his observations of the Jewish situation in Poland. But his appearance created more of a fuss than the Polish government expected. Shortly after the conference, Polish security officials urged him to leave Poland immediately. He left on August 13,

1946, for his own safety. The rabbi was whisked to the railroad station where he caught the Prague–bound train. Guards supplied by Rabbi Kahana accompanied the rabbi until the train reached the Polish–Czech border.

By August 19, 1946, UNRRA's plan for the children was ready.

Rabbi Herzog had pulled every string he could to organize a train, and have it ready to take the children out of Poland. The main agency organizing the train was UNRRA, in conjunction with the Polish Railway. UNRRA was responsible for repatriating citizens back to their native countries. A number of wounded Polish soldiers were recuperating in French hospitals. These soldiers were to be repatriated from Paris back to Warsaw. UNRRA's plan was to use the empty Polish rail train being sent empty to Paris to transport the children Rabbi Herzog wanted brought out of Poland. The train was to stop in Prague, where the children would get off and be brought to a refugee camp called Deblice. The children were to wait in Deblice until their accommodations were ready in France.

On August 19, UNRRA Prague sent a telegram to UNRRA Warsaw that the train would be available in Lodz on August 22, 1046. And it was. Drucker and Becker were there to help the children get aboard. 1 The train was to proceed to Katowice, near the Czech/Polish border, where the remainder of the children would board the train that would leave for Prague where the train was scheduled to arrive on Friday, August 23, 1946. On Wednesday, August 21,1946 at about 10 P.M. the train started to roll in the direction of Katowice where it arrived Thursday morning, August 22, 1946. In Katowice the children waited to board the train from orphanages of Bytom, Krakow and Zabrze. Drucker and the other adult escorts had their hands full watching the children waiting for the train to move. The train was waiting for the arrival of Rabbi Herzog who finally arrived late Thursday evening and the train started to roll to the Czech border. Pan Kapitan escorted the train to the Polish border where he said good bye to the children[4].

The train had several mishaps and finally reached Prague on Sunday, August 25, 1946 where the children left the train and were driven to the Deblice camp where they would remain for some time and then leave for France.

———————

## Footnotes

1. Noah Libes. Testimony at Yad Vashem p.66
2. Drucker testimony at Yad Vashem
3. Bauer, flight p.87
4. Drucker, Testimony p.69

**Chapter XII**

# Some Children Came to Zabrze
# of their own Free Will

### David Danieli

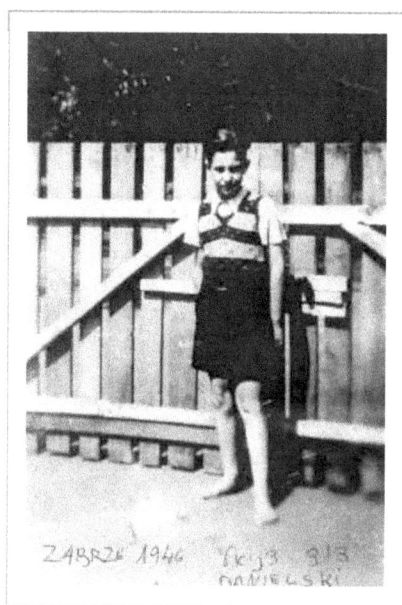

**David Danieli, formerly Daniel Danielski, at the orphanage in Zabrze in 1946**

David Danielski (surname later changed to Danieli) was born in 1932 in the hamlet of Pszczyna. His father, Max or Maximilian, was a pastry baker. The family soon moved to the bigger township of Rybnik in Silesia where Max opened a bakery in the center of the city. The bakery was very successful and the family flourished. They had a maid and their apartment was well furnished including a piano, and many antiques which David's mother, Hannah, collected. David's older brother Sasha had died in 1928 so the younger boy received a great deal of attention from Max and

Hannah. But his parents insisted that David be independent and able to defend himself when the need arose.

David does not remember much about the family or their friends. He does remember playing with other children in the courtyard of their apartment building. The family was not very religious although they belonged to the Jewish Community Center. He recalls attending very crowded services on a few occasions at the main synagogue, and his mother giving him a flag crowned with an apple to take with him to synagogue in celebration of Simchat Torah.

The new order in Germany appointed a German supervisor over the bakery, who was in essence the owner. Max Danielski was permitted to stay on at the bakery but only as a worker. Then the family was forced to move to a poorer section of the town, where other Jews were also forced to live. The new flat consisted of one room into which everything possible was moved. David's mother started to sell items from their home to provide food for the family since her husband's income became smaller with time. While selling her household items, Hannah Danielski met a German Silesian woman, Martha Kapitza, who was also involved in buying and selling goods. The transactions were highly illegal, but Hannah was able to trade her valuables for food.

Max learned from a friendly policeman that anti–Jewish actions were being planned and started to make arrangements for his son's disappearance. He contacted a Polish farmer who lived in Babia Gora who was willing to take David for a time. Hannah packed a small suitcase, gave him some pocket money and bought him a train ticket. He traveled alone to the farm. He remained with the farmer and his family for some time helping with various farm chores. On a cold night in February of 1942 the farmer took David to the station and sent him home to Rybnik. He headed home and found the apartment dark with no lights in the window. The Gestapo had posted an order on the door forbidding admittance to the premises. He had no idea what had happened to his parents and did not know what to do next having no other family in the city.

David decided to cross the street and approach the neighbor, Martha Kapitza, who had become friendly with his mother. She offered him a place to stay until things settled down. Through her, David learned that all the Jews of Rybnik including his parents were rounded up and shipped to an unknown destination. Nobody knew what happened to them. He snuck into his parents' flat through a window and found that the police had ransacked the place and made a shambles. He made two trips to his former home, carrying away as much as he could and never returned. .

Anton Kapitza, the husband of Martha Kapitza, was an out of work, disabled coal miner of Polish Silesian origin. Martha was a native of Zabrze or Hindenburg, and provided for her family by selling luxury goods in exchange for food, which she then resold. The market for these goods was excellent since there was a scarcity of finer goods in Germany during the war years. Hannah Danielski traded regularly with Martha Kapitza before she was deported and they had become good friends. Mrs. Kapitza had five children: Elizabeth who was a mute; Ernest, a soldier; Gertrude who delivered papers; Ludwig who worked in the building trades and was a bit slow; and the youngest Zigmund, born in 1933. David and Zigmund were close in age and got along pretty well. Gertrude, the oldest, born in 1923, assisted her mother in running the house and contributed financially. David did chores and errands at the direction of Martha or Gertrude Kapitza and adjusted to the situation as best he could. He knew that he was Jewish but that was about all he knew about Judaism.

Time went by and suddenly the Gestapo started searching and questioning people in the area. Apparently, someone either reported David or he heard the authorities were looking for him. Mrs. Kapitza packed a few items of clothing, gave him some money and the address of a farm supervisor in Striegau, Germany, who was originally a Polish police official. David left the house and headed for the train station just before the Gestapo arrived at the Kapitza home asking questions about his whereabouts. Gertrude later told him that her mother stated that he had left the house after stealing money. Mrs. Kapitza was even questioned at headquarters about the case but eventually the matter was dropped since she insisted that she had no knowledge of his whereabouts. Gertrude also revealed to him that her mother had promised Mrs. Danielski to help protect her son.

Meanwhile David remained with the farm supervisor helping with the chores. He started school, immediately proceeded to third grade and joined the "Hitler Jugend" or Hitler Youth, as every child belonged to the organization. He remembers collecting all kinds of materials for the war effort. One day, on the way to school, he saw for the first time people in striped pajamas who were inmates of the Gross Rosen concentration camp. He was reminded of his Jewish heritage and very worried about his parents. He would find out later that Mrs. Kapitza sent food to the Danielski's with a German who had worked with Max near Rybnik. Max died about June 16, 1942 and Mrs. Danielski was killed in Auschwitz in December 1943 at the age of 43.

By June, 1942, David had returned to the Kapitza household and taken over the newspaper route since Gertrude had married and left the house. Mrs. Kapitza managed to obtain a baptismal certificate for David and he began to attend school. He was frequently late due to the newspaper deliveries that steadily declined as the war raged against Germany. Conditions in Germany worsened each day although there was still enough food. The school building was soon converted into a military installation and classes ceased. The Russians were advancing on Germany. Being sent to the Eastern front was considered a death sentence. The Russians reached Rybnik in the winter of 1945, where they expelled the entire German population. The Kapitza family made the 40-mile trek to Zabrze where Martha's sister lived. Then the hardships really began. Anton Kapitza and David decided to head back to Rybnik and found the Kapitza home ransacked. The Russians had cleaned the place out including the basement where some food was well hidden.

Conditions were very bad The family made cookies and sold them to buy food. While dealing in the Rybnik market, David was approached by a Jewish man, Mr. Gold, who asked if he was Jewish and offered to help him return to Judaism. David felt an obligation to talk to Anton Kapitza first who saw no problem in David's learning about Judaism, Mr. Gold, who resided in Bytom, invited David to live in his home. Gold was in the process of preparing to take his family to America and asked David to join them. He agreed.

Gold also told David about the orphanage in Zabrze where he could learn about Judaism. David was sent to the orphanage, where the head teacher, David Hubel, made a great impression on him. David became an ardent Zionist, and was no longer interested in emigrating to the United States. Instead, David wanted to go to Palestine, and became very active in Zionist activities at the orphanage. The Gold family was disappointed by the decision since they really wanted to take David to the United States. They parted and never met again.

David enjoyed his stay at the orphanage where he learned the basic tenets of Judaism, Jewish history and the Hebrew language. He also attended the regular Polish school in accordance with Polish educational requirements. But David really did not devote himself to those studies since he wanted to go to Palestine. Then rumors started in the orphanage that Rabbi Herzog was coming to take all the children to Palestine.

Rabbi Itzhak Eisik Halevi Herzog, chief rabbi of the British Mandate of Palestine, received a promise from the British administration in Palestine to give entrance certificates to 500 Jewish orphans who had survived the war in Poland in monasteries, Christian homes, forests and caves. There was great excitement at the Zabrze Jewish orphanage on Karlowica Street Number 10, Zabrze, Upper Silesia, Poland, with the news of imminent departure for Palestine. Rumors chased rumors but then the children were ordered to pack. Every child began to pack his few belongings; some had smaller, others bigger suitcases. The Zabrze contingent consisted of complete orphans, partial orphans, children with one parent, children with one parent aboard the transport and children who had returned from Russia.

The following is a list of some of the Zabrze children that David Danielski could remember. In some instances the children were known merely by their nicknames.

| | |
|---|---|
| Shlomo Korn | Mrs. Wilczenski |
| Tzvi Shpigler | Renka |
| Shlomo Shpigler | Her sister |
| Yehuda Tzvi Sobol | And mother |
| Riwka Brender | Naomi Agrabska |
| Tzvi Brender | Esther Kastenberg |
| Yeizik Peitznik | Emil and mother |
| David Fridman | Big Eva |
| Hannah Hoffman | Ella |
| Rivka Motil | Roma |
| Fela Kozoch | Dwora Ditman |
| Sonia Mayer | Shmulek |
| Heniek Mayer | Batia Sheinfeld |
| Arieh | David Danieli |
| Charlotka. Brother and sister | Raya, the group leader |
| Yehudit Wilczenski | |

Some children remained at the Zabrze home with a staff headed by principal Dr. Nehema Geller and head teacher David Hubel.

David left the Zabrze home on Thursday afternoon the 22nd of August 1946. The Zabrze group first headed by tramway to the nearby town of Katowice where a train was standing on a sideline with hundreds of children, group leaders and teachers. They came from many orphanages in Poland: Lodz, Krakow, Warsaw and Katowice. The greetings, shouts and tears were beyond description. Order was soon established and the Zabrze group boarded its assigned car. Pan Kapitan, dressed in his military uniform, was there as well as Rabbi Aaron Becker. Both military chaplains had their hands full with all the logistical problems. The train and the passengers waited as time passed. It was already dark and no sign of the rabbi. The military escort of the train refused to budge. His instructions were clear, the rabbi must be aboard the train for him to give the order to move. The escorts and the children were nervous for they felt insecure in the Katowice station. Many of them heard of the violence committed against Jews along Polish railroads by Polish extreme nationalists. Trains had to be protected by soldiers or policeman against such attacks.

**Polish train protected by Polish soldiers**

The rabbi was of course finalizing the final clearance papers for his transport. He and his son were then flown from Warsaw to Katowice where they boarded the train. The Polish military commander of the transport then ordered the train to roll to the Czech border.

**Rabbi Yitzchak Isaac Herzog, Chief Rabbi of Palestine**

Late that evening the Herzog transport of children started to roll in a westerly direction toward the Czech border. The trip was slow–moving and made frequent stops, especially on the border between Poland and Czechoslovakia. Pan Kapitan and Rabbi Becker said goodbye to the children and headed back to Warsaw.

## Shlomo Koren

**Shlomo Koren at Zabrze. Shlomo Koren is a friend of David Danieli. They started their friendship at Zabrze and maintain it to this day. Shlomo was kind enough to write his life story for us in Hebrew and we translated it to English.**
This picture was provided by the "Lochamei Hagetaot" Museum

I, Shlomo Koren was born in Nowy Sacz, Galicia Poland and survived World War II in Russia, returning to Poland following the war in 1946. My family settled in Katowice, Poland, where I was registered in a city public school but did not attend classes. I barely spoke Polish. I met David Danieli (Danielski) in Katowice. He told me that he was attending a Jewish school in Zabrze, about a half hour away, and invited me to visit him. I visited the Zabrze home on several occasions and was pleased by the ambience of the place. I liked the home, especially the individual attention that the place gave the children. I discussed the situation with my mother and sisters. I had no father. The family had difficulty controlling me and I often roamed the streets of Katowice, so they consented to my moving to the home. The orphanage readily accepted me, for the institution was specifically created for children like me.

**Notice the picture of Shlomo in the second line from the bottom. The picture is numbered 76. (Actually, it looks like 76 but is really the Hebrew letters, tet and vav which equal fifteen. Notice that the little girl is Yod, gimel 13, the boy next to her is Yod, dalet – 14)**

At Zabrze, I was in a room with two other boys; one of them named Morin Landau. Each of us had experienced horrible events that we tried to forget. Some of the girls at the home spoke only Polish and continued to pray and cross themselves, refusing to admit that they were Jewish. The teachers and supervisors had a difficult time reaching some of the children but with time managed to win their confidence and provide them with a basic education and a bit of self–confidence. Jewish religious education was introduced in moderation so as not to antagonize the children who were ill at ease, if not hostile, to anything Jewish. The boys were taught how to pray, put on phylacteries, just as the girls were taught about lighting candles and all children were exposed to Jewish holidays and a bit of a Jewish atmosphere. Hebrew, Jewish history, and Zionism were stressed at the home.

Within the compound of the Jewish community at Zabrze near the orphanage, there was also a building where a group of young pioneers were preparing themselves to move to Palestine and work the land. The group or kibbutz belonged to the Ichud Zionist movement. We watched the youngsters frequently dancing "horas" and other folk dances in the yard of the compound and were impressed. Their enthusiasm inspired us to become more fervent Zionists. After four months of ideal life at the home, we heard that Rabbi Herzog was coming to take us to Palestine. I began to beg my mother and sisters to permit me to leave Poland with the others. They were not opposed to Palestine but feared the distance and the unknown. Slowly and persistently I managed to convince them that I must go to Palestine. Mother bought me a new jacket, shoes and stitched some dollars into my pants in case of an emergency.

Time flew and we left the home and headed to Katowice, Poland, where we boarded a train with other youngsters. The train waited for the arrival of Rabbi Herzog and his entourage. He arrived late in the evening and the train started to roll to the Czech border. The next day was Friday, the train stopped and we spent Shabbat at a hotel in Moravski–Ostrava. There was a bit of chaos at the hotel since the children made great use of the hotel telephones, elevators and borrowed items that were never returned.

On Sunday, the train resumed the journey to Prague where we disembarked and were taken to a refugee camp named Repatrianski Tabor Dablice to await entrance visas to France. We would remain in this camp for about six weeks. Our Zabrze group became part of the Hapoel Hamizrahi group. The group leaders were not well disposed to our Zabrze contingent since we spoke primarily Polish and were less familiar with Jewish customs than the Mizrahi group. A certain distance existed between the groups. The Zabrze group was very sensitive and received a great deal of attention at the home due to our origins and experiences while the regular Mizrahi youths were familiar with Jewish life. The Mizrahi youth leaders also lacked the necessary educational tools to handle the sensitive Zabrze contingent. Still, a routine was established at the refugee camp and we youngsters had to abide by it.

Some of us boys, including David Danieli, soon formed a group that would travel to Prague and spend time in the city. I sold my stamp collection in Prague in order to have spending money. We went to the movies and saw many city attractions in Prague. I was displeased with our group leader and joined a group of boys that raided the youth warehouse following dinner on the first night of Rosh Hashanah. We took clothing and food and gave it all out to the children, who appeared at services the next day at in brand new outfits. The group leaders could do little about our antics.

The French visas arrived a day after Rosh Hashanah. We headed to the railway station, boarded a train and traveled for the next two days across Germany until we reached Strasbourg, France. We were taken to the Strasbourg Jewish community service center, where we spent the holidays. We were then moved to a three–story house on Rue Selenic in the center of Strasbourg that belonged to the Jewish community. The main floor had halls that were converted into a synagogue, dining room and study centers. The second floor consisted of dorms and the third floor had small rooms for the staffers and their families. The place was crowded and disorganized. The group leaders became a bit more tyrannical in their behavior toward us. Discipline was strictly enforced and offenders were given cleaning chores as punishment. Soon the younger children were removed to a home in Schirmeck, making life at the home a bit easier.

Some of us were not pleased with the management at the home and expressed it openly. The administration then made arrangements to move nine of us to the Jewish orphanage of Strasbourg administered by Mr. and Mrs. Blum. The Blum's gave us a warm reception with plenty of tasty food, some clothing, bed sheets and transportation passes. We were assigned to an American ORT program where we were taught various trades. I selected courses in metal work. The instruction was primarily in German but

I also received instruction in French. All children had to attend services at the synagogue of Rabbi Deutch of Strasbourg.

I had ample time to enjoy the city and meet with my friends who remained at the home in Rue Selenic. But I was restless and anxious to head to Palestine. I started to talk to the other boys of the transport and we soon formed a group that was determined to make aliyah. We approached the children from the home on Selenic with our plan and some youngsters joined us, including David Danieli. We had neither the money nor the connections to carry out our plan. David decided to write a letter to his friend, David Hubel, the headmaster in Zabrze, explaining our problem and asking for help.

The answer soon came in the form of train tickets and a date of departure to Marseilles, France. We packed and bid farewell to our temporary homes. The Selenic Street home threw a party in our honor and we left for Marseilles where an emissary met us and took us to an isolated and empty house. We remained there until Passover and then moved to another camp facing the sea. Here preparations were being made for the departure of the next illegal ship. Hundreds of boarding passes were forged with the South American country of Columbia as the destination. Then one night, Jewish refugees began to arrive en masse and were organized in groups and sent to board the ship, Exodus. Our group was one of the last to board the very crowded ship.

On July 11, 1947, the ship managed to leave the docking berth without a pilot and headed out to sea. The British navy followed the ship and then rammed the boat on the high seas. Fights ensued between the British boarding parties and the immigrants resulting in the death of three civilians, among them an American sailor, and dozens of seriously wounded passengers. The illegal ship was brought to Haifa where all passengers were transferred to three prison ships and started their voyage back to France.

The French refused to force the passengers off the boats and eventually the ships sailed to Hamburg where we docked on September 6, 1947. Our ship, the "*Empire Rival*", was the last ship to dock and we were immediately placed aboard a train and transported to Lubeck where trucks took us to the camp called Amstau. We were later transferred to another camp named Pependorf where there were more youngsters. Here we participated in various activities and also studied Hebrew. Soon we began to travel in the direction of France under the leadership of "Brichah" agents and eventually made it back to Strasbourg. The home at Rue Selenic was closed and Mr. Blum was happy to see the group. I continued my train trip to Marseilles where I entered a huge refugee camp named "Grand Arnas."

**The Exodus ship arriving in the port of Haifa, Palestine**

**The Exodus passengers forced to leave the train in Germany. British military trucks would transport them to D.P. camps in the British military zone in Germany**

The camp contained many nationalities including Jews waiting for visas for America or residence papers to stay in France. Within a week we were transferred to the Jewish Agency camp "Villa Gabi," a beautiful place overlooking the sea. Here we awaited an illegal ship that would take us to Palestine. Then came the order that only volunteers for the Israeli Army would be sent to Israel. I was informed that I would be sent back to the Rue Selenic orphanage that had now moved to the Chateau Voisin near Paris. I refused to go back to the home and joined a Hagana training camp in the vicinity of Marseilles. I lied about my age, told them I was 18 and was accepted for military training. I then boarded a ship with Canadian volunteers and landed in Haifa toward the end of May 1948. I was immediately sent to the "Yona" military base near Beit Lid and within a few days, I was ordered to assemble with the other soldiers. I must have looked younger than the other soldiers because when the commander saw me, he told me to return my weapon and wait for him. Following the formation, he dropped me off at the immigrant hostel in Raanana on his way to visit his parents. Thus ended my wanderings from 1939 to 1948.

## Klara Frauenglass

Below is a translation of a Polish weitten document describing the life of Klara. The document itself is in very poor condition and had to be translated. Originally translated from Polish to English by Iwo Bialynicki–Birula, Eva Mihokova and Richard Kerner.

Document No 1023 composed by Mrs. W. Berkelhamer

Nursery in Zabrze

August 11, 1946

Little Klarcia, wonderful black–haired creature, looking like a little Japanese child, all the time stands near and cuddles up to me, yearning for tenderness. When I gave her a mirror, she was so happy, she held out her cheek to be kissed, and hid the mirror in the pocket of her apron.

The history of this child was told to me by Dr. Necha Geller.

Klarcia Frauenglas was born in Zbaraz (*Eastern Galicia*) in 1941. (*The Germans steadily reduced the Jewish population by massive actions of killing and deportations. The parents decided to entrust their child to a Polish acquaintance hoping that she would keep the child under her protection.*)

In 1943, before the final Action, the parents gave the child to a Polish woman; the parents were killed during the Action. After the Action, the woman brought the child to the Gestapo and the girl was condemned to death by shooting. A Gestapo officer took aim but little Klarcia, a very lively child, imagined that he was playing with her; she was jumping and with her little hand knocked the revolver out of his hand. The officer tried once and twice and finally gave up.

He handed the revolver to a Ukrainian militiaman and ordered him to shoot her. And what do you know, the same thing happened. The Ukrainian took aim but the child knocked the revolver again out of his hand. All present were amazed and exclaimed in German that it was a miracle. "Ein Kind, dass die Kugel nicht greifen will" (*A child that the bullet can't hit*).

They decided that the child must live. The Gestapo chief summoned the Ukrainian mayor of Zbaraz and told him to keep the child alive. The mayor sent the child to the local Ukrainian orphanage. She remained there throughout the war and was saved.

About three months ago, a Polish repatriated woman from Zbaraz brought the girl to the Zabzre orphanage and left her there.. When she arrived, she didn't know a word of Polish, she only spoke Ukrainian. Now she talks Polish and socializes with the other children. She is a darling of the entire orphanage.

In Zbaraz all Jews and Catholics were familiar with the story of the miraculously saved Jewish child.

Zabrze, Aug 11, 1946

Dr. Geller

*Originally translated from Polish to English by Iwo Bialynicki–Birula, Eva Mihokova and Richard Kerner.*

**Apage of pictures from the Drucker album sent to us by** the "Ghetto Fighters' House", a history museum commemorating those who fought the Nazis.

**First line. Left to Right. Picture 2, Marked with the Hebrew letter " B" bet, is Klara Frauenglass. Klara Frauenglass left Poland reached France and then sailed to Israel with other children**

The kibbutz Ghetto Fighters' operates the Ghetto Fighters' House, a history museum commemorating those who fought the Nazis. The kibbutz was founded in 1949 on the coastal highway between Acre and Nahariya, on the site of abandoned British Army base[2] and depopulated Palestinian village of al-Sumayriyya.[3]Its founding members include surviving fighters of the Warsaw Ghetto Uprising(notably Icchak Cukierman, ŻOB deputy commander), as well as former Jewish partisans and other Holocaust survivors. Its name commemorates the Jews who fought the Nazis. Adjacent to the museum is a large amphitheater used frequently for concerts, assemblies, and ceremonies hosted by the museum. Alongside the kibbutz are the extensive remains of an aqueduct which supplied water to Acre some 6 km away, until 1948. The aqueduct was originally built at the end of the 18th century by Jezzar Pasha, the Ottoman ruler of Acre, but was completely rebuilt by his son, Suleiman, in 1814.

*We would like to take this opportunity to thank the museum for all the help that was extended to us.*

**Chapter XIII**

# Forceful Redemption Cases

## Pradnik District in Krakow

In the city of Krakow, there is a district named Pradnik. There is also a river by the same name that crosses Krakow. In this area of the suburb, there was a pub that was owned by a disabled woman who was born with deformed legs and moved about in a wheel chair pushed by a helper[1]. One day she was sitting near the Pradnik river and noticed that a woman had attached a stone to the neck of the child and lowered and raised the child above the water. The infant was a tiny toddler of about two or three months. Apparently, the woman was trying to drown the baby but could not go through with it. The disabled woman asked her helper to push the wheel chair in the direction of the woman. She immediately saw that the woman was Jewish. She asked the Jewish woman what she was doing with the baby, the latter replied that her situation was hopeless and she could not support the child. She also told the disabled woman that the baby was actually her sister's who was rounded up in an action. She managed to leave the baby with her sister. The latter kept the baby for a while but presently she reached the end of her rope and decided to end the baby's sufferings. The disabled woman asked the Jewish woman whether she can have the infant and she would care for her. The Jewish woman was startled. She had nothing to give the woman that was taking a great risk. If caught by the Germans she would not ever get out alive. The Jewish woman had no choice and handed the baby over to the helper who in turn placed the child in the arms of the disabled woman who looked at the angelic face of the small infant. She told the Jewish woman that she was the owner of the pub and invited her to her place of business.

The pub attracted local Polish residents and also German soldiers stationed in the area. One of the German soldiers took a liking to the child and devoted a great deal of time to the infant. He even took the child for walks and bought gifts for her. The owner told everybody that the child belonged to her family and was sent to her since her father was a Polish officer who was killed in the Polish–German war in 1939. The mother disappeared without leaving a trace. The child was sent to the disabled woman. The locals accepted the story but in 1942, the Gestapo issued an ordinance who everybody that took care of children must have baptismal certificates. She had no official papers for the baby. She went from church to church and tried to get a certificate and told all kind of stories but no one issued a certificate. Finally, one old priest told her that her stories are nonsense and that she had a Jewish child with her. When she admitted the fact, he issued a baptismal certificate for the child.

The Jewish woman survived the war and returned to Krakow. She went to the pub and asked the owner for the child. The disabled women refused to hand over the child. The woman came to Pan Kapitan for help. She also revealed a stunning story. Her sister was meeting and seeing a German soldier. The soldier helped her. She gave birth to their child. The soldier kept supporting her sister and the baby. Then the sister was sent to a concentration camp where the soldier could no longer help her. He did help in sending the child to the sister prior to the deportation. The German soldier recognized the baby in the pub and paid special attention to the child until his unit was moved.

The sister wanted her niece back but the owner of the pub refused to listen. She was not interested in money. She loved the child and treated her well. The child refused to leave the place. Pan Kapitan felt bad about the case since the disabled woman risked her life to save the infant and provided her with a good home. True, the aunt also had a claim. Pan Kapitan had to make a decision that he felt would be wrong either way.

Suddenly the case took a total unexpected turn. The Polish authorities accused the owner of the pub of co–operating with the Germans during the war. This was a very serious charge that could result in years of prison and loss of all possessions. The woman was desperate and sought help but few people wanted to involve themselves in such cases. She called on Pan Kapitan who spoke to Rabbi Kahana. The Jewish religious association of Krakow composed a letter to the effect that the owner of the pub was friendly with the Germans since she was hiding a Jewish child. Attached to the letter was the statement of the aunt attesting that she gave the child to the disabled woman who kept the child throughout the war. All these papers were prepared under one condition that the child would be returned to the aunt with the end of the proceedings. The papers were filed and the Jewish religious association pressured the legal instances to speed up the proceedings. The charges were dropped; the girl went with aunt. The disabled woman continued her business.

## The Hungarian Jewish Boy

Hungarian Jewish transports began to arrive in Auschwitz in March, 1944. One of the passengers was a woman with a circumcised boy[2]. Yeshayahu does not know too much about the mother who shared a bunk with a Polish woman. The woman survived the camp and returned home with the Jewish boy. The father of the boy survived the war and searched everywhere for his son. He came to Drucker and presented all the necessary papers that showed the boy belonged to him. He even knew the name of the Polish woman and where she lived. He went to her place and asked for his son. The woman refused to talk to him and practically threw him out of her place. It later appeared that the boy contributed to her income.

The Central Committee office of Polish Jews in Krakow publicized a sheet that told Poles that they can return Jewish children to Jewish orphanages or they can keep them at home and receive a monthly payment for the maintenance of the Jewish child. We already mentioned earlier that the Central Committee of Polish Jews was not interested in removing Jewish children from non–Jewish homes unless there were special problems. The woman in this case received a monthly payment for the boy. All attempts to talk to her proved futile. Pan Kapitan decided to follow the woman and the boy in the morning and see where the boy goes to school. Pan Kapitan followed and recorded the name of the school. He then took the father who was a Hungarian citizen to the Hungarian embassy where he obtained all necessary papers attesting to the child being a Hungarian citizen. With these papers they proceeded to the Polish Ministry of Interior, which ordered that the child be returned to the father. Hungary and Poland were on very friendly relations then and all legal problems were expedited. Pan Kapitan and the Hungarian father requested that a police officer escort them to the school where the boy was studying. The group entered the school and went to the principal's office. They presented all legal papers and asked for the boy to be brought to the office. The principal did not like what he saw but the papers, the police officer and Pan Kapitan dressed in his military uniform convinced him to settle the matter.

The boy came to the office and was introduced to his father who took him by the hand. The group left the school. Father and son headed to Zabrze for a few days and then left for Hungary.

**Seated from left to right: Dr. Nechema Geller (with purse at her feet) and David Hubel. One of the children at this celebration was Edzio Rosenblatt.**

The Zabrze orphanage not only accepted youngsters but also had a toddler section as shown by this photograph. The photo was taken during one of the festivals that the home organized to acquaint the children with their Jewish heritage.

Pan Kapitan worked very hard to redeem the child and return him to his mother. Chaya Garn was born in Radomysl in 1921 to Chaim Leib Garn, the son of Benyamin Garn of Wielki Most in the Mielec district near Rzeszow. The Garn family were successful merchants. Chaya was one of six daughters. Two of her sisters left Poland for France prior to World War II. On September 8, 1939, following weak Polish military resistance, German soldiers entered Radomysl. They immediately began to harass Jews, especially Jewish men who were forced into work details or sent to the Pustkow labor camp near Debice, helping build a new S.S. military training base. Some Jews managed to escape Pustkow but most died there. The Germans also carried out house–to–house searches, ostensibly looking for weapons, but in reality using the searches as excuses to loot the Jewish apartments. The German authorities installed a "Judenrat" or a council of Jewish leaders, in Radomysl mainly to carry out the Gestapo's orders to provide cheap Jewish labor to Pustkow. In one action in November 1940, 700 Jews of Radomysl were rounded up and sent to Pustkow. Before long, just breathing the word "Pustkow" terrified any Jew within earshot. Awraham Rosenblatt, originally from the town of Oswiecim (Auschwitz), came to Radomysl where he heard life was relatively better than in other Polish towns. He met and married Chaya Garn. But in July, 1942, a few weeks after Awraham and Chaya were married, the Germans ordered the registration of the entire Jewish population of Radomysl. Special identity cards were issued to young skilled workers, among them the young

Rosenblatt couple. Supposedly these cards carried with them some measure of protection from being shipped off to Pustkow. Awraham and Chaya were smart enough not to trust the Germans. The young couple made arrangements for themselves and Chaya's parents to hide outside the city in the house of a Polish farmer.

One Saturday night they all quietly snuck out of Radomysl, reaching the house of Tomas Szczurek in the village of Dulca Wielki. It was a lucky move. The next day, while they hid out in Szczurek's farm, the Jews of Radomysl were all rounded up, faced the dreaded "selection" process and were deported to concentration camps.

The next day, Sunday, Szczurek's wife was in church where she heard rumors the Germans were searching for Jews. She rushed home terrified, knowing that hiding Jews carried the death penalty. She immediately ordered the Rosenblatts out of the house, but relented slightly when they begged for a few more hours. That night the Rosenblatts slipped off into the fields, heading for nearby Dombrowa. In exchange for the risks they took, the Szczureks kept most of the Rosenblatts' belongings.

Jews could not use the main road for fear of discovery and arrest, so Awraham and Chaya and her parents stumbled over difficult paths, uneven fields and undulating meadows. The fields were beautiful in the sunlight with the light refreshing breeze, but torture for these city folks plodding through mud and rocky cowpats.

The group finally reached Dombrowa where they sought shelter and a much needed rest. But the Nazi "actions," shootings and searches forced them to keep moving. But where? Which direction? Danger lurked around every bend in the road.

Chaya turned to a Polish friend, a bureaucrat with the Polish government who worked in Mielec. In Dombrowa she used a telephone in a Polish stranger's home and called her friend. Again, luck seemed to be on her side. Her friend told her he'd send a truck to pick her up the next day. That's as far as her luck held. When she hung up the phone, her Polish benefactor, who had overheard the conversation, warned her that staying in Dombrowa was impossible. The Nazis were planning an anti–Jewish "action" in Dombrowa the next day, probably before the truck would arrive. The family hired a trusted guide and reluctantly left Dombrowa, looking over their shoulders. They snuck into the Jewish ghetto in Tarnow, where they found a place to stay and some work. Then they were forced to flee to the forest as the Nazis began their roundup of Jews in Tarnow.

Fugitives, they hid in the woods, living in caves, taking their lives in their hands when they snuck into a farmer's yard to buy some food.

Winter was fast approaching, the leaves had turned yellow and some of the trees were already barren. When the chill wind blew, it carried a hint of the harsh winter close behind. And Chaya discovered she was pregnant. It was one thing to be pregnant in a city or even village, where a hospital or midwife could help with the birth. But they were in hiding, dodging the Nazis who still roamed the area, constantly exposed to danger. Even if the baby were delivered successfully, and both mother and child were healthy, what then? Who would take care of the infant? Chaya, undernourished, weak and sick, was in no position to nurse a child or even care for one.

They found shelter with a family named Kokoszka. But when their hosts discovered Chaya was pregnant, they were evicted. A pregnant woman could not sprint away and hide from Nazis if they showed up to search the house. Again, the Rosenblatts were reduced to begging not only for their own lives, but for that of the as yet unborn child.

The Kokoszkas were not bad people. They had already risked their lives allowing the Rosenblatts to stay in the drafty, cold attic. They then mercifully took an even bigger risk: they allowed the Rosenblatts to remain, temporarily. On the evening of January 4, 1944, Chaya was lowered from the attic and taken to the stable. There, on

January 5, 1944, on a blanket covering a thin layer of straw, Chaya, perhaps because of her weakened condition, strained terribly but still gave birth to a healthy baby boy. But Chaya was anything but healthy. She lost consciousness and was carried delirious back to the attic. She did not recover consciousness

for several days. During that time both the Rosenblatts and the Kokoszkas knew only drastic measures could be taken. The infant was cleansed and swaddled. A note hung from the baby's wrist stating falsely that his name was Edzio and that he had been baptized. Then the infant was wrapped in a blanket and placed on the windowsill of a Polish farmer named Jozef Balczyniak.

That night in January was bitter cold. Balczyniak's wife thought she heard the house cats meowing at the door, begging to come in from the freezing outdoors. She told her husband to open the door and let the poor cats into the house. He spotted a bundle on one of the windowsills and realized immediately that it was a baby. Their ten–year old daughter thought the baby adorable, even if he was crying. Balczyniak's wife was suspicious. She pointed angrily at her husband, accusing him of being the father. At the time, farm girls were known to abandon a baby they could not or did not want to take care of. But Balczyniak denied any connection to the baby. Then they discovered the note with the child's name and that he'd been baptized. The Balcyzyniaks decided to wait until morning before making any decisions. The hungry infant wailed through the night. While the Balcyzyniaks had milk in the cupboard they had no bottle to feed the child. But maternal instincts run strong. Mrs. Balcyzyniak cuddled the infant, trying to sooth him to sleep. In the morning the Balcyzyniaks trekked down to the local police station and told the police they'd found a baby on their windowsill. "Keep him or get rid of him," the policeman told them. "I don't care. This isn't a matter for the police."

The Balcyzyniaks brought the baby home.

Mrs. Balcyzyniak took pity on the child. She'd found a bottle and fed the child properly and decided to keep him. Not sure of his baptism, they had him baptized formally and legally adopted the child, officially registering him as Stanislaw Dulecki, in honor of the town's mayor. But they continued to call him Edzio, the name that was on the note attached to his wrist when they found him, the name his birth parents knew him by.

As an example of how life can change minute by minute, from smiles to tears, Chaya Rosenblatt finally regained consciousness, weak, feverish, wanting to see her baby. How do you tell a woman that her baby was no longer there? "No longer there," she asked, shocked.

Groggy. Was the baby dead? No, not dead. Gone. Gone? Gone? Yes, gone. Safe. Well–fed. Cared for. But gone.

Minutes passed slowly as Chaya accepted the harsh reality: she no longer had a baby. A few days later, their host, Mr. Kokoszka, came back from town with more unpleasant surprises. Kokoszka's son had received an order from the Germans in charge of the area that he was to leave immediately for Germany where he was needed as a laborer. But Kokoszka's son decided to ignore the orders, dangerously defying the Germans. Kokoszka was wise enough to know that this defiance would incite the Germans to search for Kokoszka's son and punish him. Through his act of rebellion, Kokoszka's son had invited the wrath of the German authorities down on the village and all who lived there. Having few options, even though Chaya was running a high fever, the Rosenblatts had to leave. Knowing Jews were already hiding in the forest, Kokoszka volunteered to help. He backed his old mare into the carriage he used to carry supplies to town and laid Chaya tenderly on the cracked, thinly padded seat of the carriage, helping the Rosenblatts flee to the forest. Over the summer of 1944, the Red Army made significant advances, liberating the towns of Mielec, Radomysl and even half of Dulcze. But the Germans beat them back. With snow already on the ground, large contingents of German troops poured into the forest with orders to capture or shoot whoever they found, especially partisans who'd fought against them, and Jews. The Jews' forest hideout was quickly discovered by German soldiers. Awraham Rosenblatt tried to run but was cut down by German marksmen. The other forest Jews were captured and sent to the death camp of Plaszow near Krakow. In the Plaszow camp, with the exception of Chaya Rosenblatt and two other Jewish women, the forest Jews of Radomysl were all murdered.

As the Soviets advanced, prisoners of Plaszow were lined up and marched at gunpoint through the ice and snow in the direction of the Bergen Belsen concentration camp. This death march went on for 14 days. Only 40% of those who began the march reached Bergen Belsen alive. Chaya Rosenblatt was shoved into a Bergen Belsen barrack with 800 other inmates in a space that was meant for 50. When the British army liberated Bergen Belsen in May 1945, Chaya had a severe case of typhus and was struggling to stay alive. British doctors hospitalized her immediately. Her recovery was painfully slow. When she could finally be moved, the British sent Chaya on a ship to Sweden.

As Chaya recovered, she looked back on what she'd gone through, the memory of her baby foremost in her mind. Chaya knew the child was still in Poland, living with the Balczyniak family in the area of Radomysl. Among the different organizations and people she sought to help her retrieve the child was an influential Swedish Jew named Paul Olberg in Stockholm. He replied to Chaya's inquiries in Yiddish. Olberg directed Chaya Rosenblatt to contact the "Bund" office in Lodz, Poland. She did but nothing happened.

She then contacted the office of the Chief Rabbi of the Polish Army, Rabbi Kahane, and told him the story. The case was handed over to Yeshayahu Drucker. Chaya Rosenblatt also learned to her chagrin that obtaining the release of Jewish children from Christian families or institutions, especially once the child had been baptized, was both a difficult and expensive procedure.

A distant relative of Chaya Rosenblatt wrote her that she had seen Edzio in Poland. Determined to retrieve her son, but still too weak to return to Poland, Chaya headed to France, to her sisters who had survived the war. From France she contacted the Jewish community office in Mielec, Poland. Chaya's letter was perused by most of the Mielec Jewish survivors. Coincidentally, one of the Mielec survivors owned a piece of land that he wanted to sell. He immediately realized that this was an opportunity to sell the land.

Mr. Balcyzyniak, the farmer who had taken in the Rosenblatt baby, wanted to buy the property from the Jew, but could not come up with the cash. So a plan was devised. Chaya would raise the money for Balcyzyniak in exchange for the baby, and Balcyzyniak would pay the Jewish landowner, who would use the money to get out of Poland.

Pan Kapitan visited the child and brought him candies and toys at the remote Balcyzyniak farm. Each time Balcyzyniak and his wife refused to give up the child. Pan Kapitan formulated an expensive plan and estimated that he would have to pay Balcyzyniak about $2,000 to free Chaya's son. Chaya, of course, did not have $2,000, or anywhere near it. But an American journalist named Reuven Island suggested he help her write her war experiences for the New York Yiddish daily newspaper *Der Tog*. Perhaps that would help. Chaya agreed. The articles ran from June 16, 1946, to July 5, 1946. The last article ended with a plea in Yiddish for contributions. Chaya received the fee from the newspaper articles as well as the money raised from the fundraising campaign.

The headline for the ad read: "A FUND IS BEING CREATED IN ORDER TO RANSOM THE CHILD OF CHAYA GARN– ROSENBLATT." The story beneath the headline explained: "A committee has been established to help Chaya Garn–Rosenblatt ransom her child from non–Jewish hands. A drive is being started to create a fund to help this holy cause. Contributions can be sent to the â€˜Fund.'

"All contributions must be sent to the Chaya Garn–Rosenblatt Fund, c/o The Day, 183 East Broadway, New York 2, N.Y."

The money was transferred to Pan Kapitan.

At the time, Rabbi Kahane's office used a rubber stamp for official documents. The top of the stamp read, "The Polish Army, general headquarters." Beneath this heading, in smaller letters, "military rabbinate." Drucker was in the habit of only applying the upper half of this rubber stamp when using it on official documents. He wrote a letter in formal Polish army terminology that the "Polish Army was interested in restoring the child located at the Balczyniak farm near

Radomysl to his biological mother." Neither the child's mother nor her place of residence was mentioned. The letter was signed in the formal manner with the appropriate stamp, lacking the "military rabbinate" line. Without any prior notice, Captain Drucker presented himself at the police station in Radomysl dressed in his officer's uniform with a hat that had a rim similar to the one worn by the Polish U.B. (Urzad Bezpieczenstwa – Office of Public Security or Polish secret police). Pan Kapitan slammed the letter on the desk of the chief of police. When the Radomysl chief of police looked up and saw Pan Kapitan in his quasi-Polish secret police hat, carrying an official letter with the Polish army stamp, he was terrified. He treated the affair as official Polish business of the highest level. The police chief glanced over the letter as Pan Kapitan told him, "We know that the farmer has incurred considerable expense raising the child. And he is to be repaid in full." Drucker then laid a brown paper package on the table. "Here is a package containing more than one million zlotys (about $2,500, a huge amount of money in those days) that will be left with you so that the farmer can buy himself the farm a Jew is offering for sale if he releases the child." The Jewish survivor who wanted to sell the farm to Balczyniak was conveniently present at the police station.

The local police chief was so distraught by the scene that he sent two policemen to bring the farmer and the boy to the station. Balczyniak arrived carrying the two–year old boy. When the police chief tried to explain the situation, Balczyniak refused to listen. The police chief then strongly hinted that he had the means to force Balczyniak to accept the deal. Balczyniak, frightened by the threat, finally realized he had no choice but to release the boy. He received the package of money in return. At this point the Jewish owner of the farmland entered the room and Balczyniak gave him the package of money. Balczyniak now owned a farm but no longer had a son, even if the boy was not really his.

Pan Kapitan scooped up the boy, left the police station, slid into his Polish army car, the motor already running, and drove away, heading toward Krakow. During the trip from Radomysl to Krakow, Pan Kapitan spoke with the boy, who already knew him from Drucker's previous visits. The youngster asked Drucker, "Uncle, do you have a rifle?" "No," Pan Kapitan answered, "but I have a gun. Why do you ask? Why do I need a rifle?" "In order to kill Jews," answered the boy. Other than that revealing conversation, the trip was uneventful. The car reached Krakow safely. Drucker headed straight for the home of his younger brother Aaron, who had married after the war and settled in Krakow. Pan Kapitan took the boy and bought him some clothing since the farmer had not packed clothing for the child. He then took a picture of the child and send it to Edzio's mother in Paris who has never seen the child.

Edzio (Stanislaw) Rosenblatt, Krakow, Poland 1946. The picture was dated December 17, 1946. An inscription was written on the back, reading "I do not know you, dear mother, who sacrificed herself so much for me, your son." Signed, "Stanislaw." The note was written in Polish

The boy was free at last, but still in Poland. Chaya was still in Paris. Somehow Pan Kapitan had to close the gap.

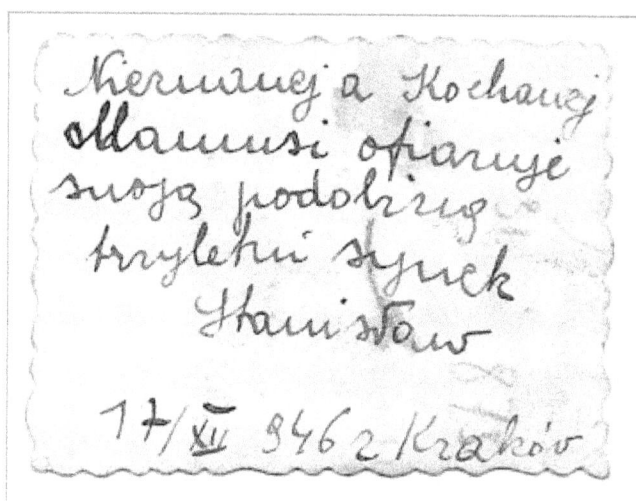

**Polish inscription on the back of the photo**

Meanwhile Pan Kapitan took Edzio Rosenblatt to the Jewish orphanage at Zabrze where Edzio was the youngest child. He quickly became the favorite of not only the teachers but also the other children who treated him as a beloved mascot.

Like the other children at Zabrze, Edzio awaited a way to leave Poland for Palestine. Most of these children left Poland; some legally and others illegally. The "Brichah" or escape movement transported most of the older children to the displaced person camps in Germany or Austria. Some transports of children went directly to France. The children's transports that left Poland usually combined children from different Jewish orphanages: religious, secular, Zionist or non–Zionist, including the children of Zabrze.

As a rule, the children were assembled in the city of Lodz, which had the largest Jewish population in postwar Poland. No sooner had Edzio "Stanislaw" Rosenblatt arrived in Zabrze than preparations were begun for his departure. Being a very small child, he needed special care and attention. As the necessary preparations were made, Pan Kapitan sent a letter to Chaya Rosenblatt in Polish informing her that her son Edzio would be leaving Poland and hopefully would join her soon in Paris. Edzio left Poland with a transport of Jewish children for France. Pan Kapitan sent a cable to Chaya informing her that Edzio had left Poland. Mother and son would soon be united.

**Zabrze staff and children at a Lag B'Omer celebration**

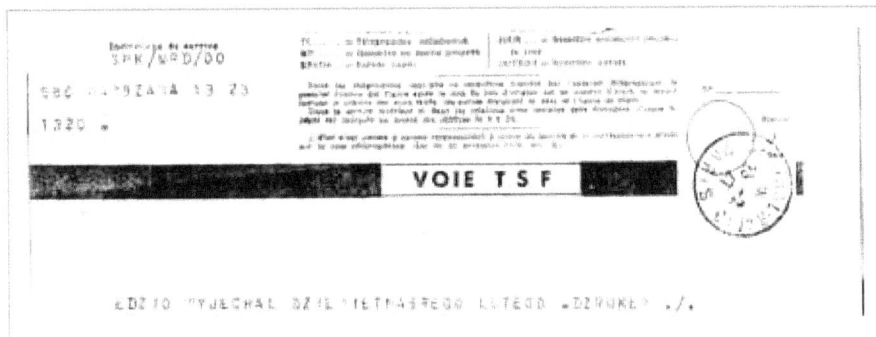

**Pan Kapitan's cable to Edzio's mother in Paris**

## Footnotes

1. Drucker, Testimony pp.44–49
2. Drucker, Testimony pp 29–50

## Chapter XIV

# The Dismantlement of Jewish life in Eastern Europe

Parliamentary elections were held in Poland on January 19, 1947, the first since World War II. According to the official results, the Democratic Bloc (*Blok Demokratyczny*), dominated by the communist Polish Workers Party (PPR), gained 80.1% of the vote and 394 of the 444 seats in the legislative Sejm of Poland. The resulting government was a communist–dominated government that began to take matters in hand. The various government security and police forces were increased throughout the country. Their powers were vastly increased. The opposition was dismantled, harassed and decimated. The Communist Party was on the way to establishing itself as the only party in Poland.

The Polish borders were closed and the police began to check the various activities of Jewish organizations, especially the Zionist organizations. There was nothing specific, but the feeling of being watched was in evidence everywhere and made people ill at ease, especially Zionist officials. Drucker continued to redeem Jewish children from non–Jewish homes although he had to be more careful because the Polish administration began to tighten rules and follow procedures. The redemption prices of Jewish children also increased and put a strain on Jewish financial reserves. The Zionist homes continued to function but at a reduced level since their residents were sent abroad.

One day, Pan Kapitan, as Drucker became known, received a letter from the kibbutz Evron in Palestine stating that the son of the writer's sister was wandering through Poland. [1] The letter stated that the writer was already an elderly person and would like to rescue the child but knew little of his whereabouts in Poland. By pure chance, Pan Kapitan had picked a Jewish boy in the village of Garbolin in the area of Warsaw. It appeared that the boy had been handed over by his Jewish parents to a Polish family for safe-keeping, but the family chased the boy away from their house. The child wandered about the streets of Warsaw and lived with a gang of children that dealt in cigarettes on the streets of Warsaw. During the Polish revolt in Warsaw, in

1944, the child escaped with Poles out of the city and they ran to the countryside. The child was tired and fell asleep at a farm in Garbolin. The farmer picked him up and gave him shelter until the end of the war. Pan Kapitan had received information about the child and visited the farmer several times but the Pole refused to surrender the child. Pan Kapitan continued to pressure the farmer who finally consented to release the child. He then asked the farmer for the name of the child. The farmer replied that the child was known as Bazem Barnowicz. Pan Kapitan asked the farmer to bring the child to the chaplaincy office in Warsaw where the farmer would be paid in exchange for the child. The farmer sent his wife with the child to the office in Warsaw. Pan Kapitan waited for them and asked the boy to step into a room next door and Pan Kapitan gave the woman the money. She started to count as the boy peeked in and saw the money being counted. He screamed: "You are selling me for money." She threw the money on the floor and went to take the boy. Pan Kapitan assembled the money and put it into her bag and gently pushed her out of the room. He kept the boy, who was crying. Pan Kapitan told the boy that he was his "uncle." He talked and talked and calmed the child who was taken to the orphanage in Zabrze. Pan Kapitan kept talking to the boy hoping to find some clue as to his identity.

Pan Kapitan decided to take the boy to Warsaw and walk with him in the area where the children who sold cigarettes used to hang about. The boy recognized the streets and even remembered the place from where he had been kicked out. He even told Drucker the apartment where he had lived. Pan Kapitan returned to the building dressed in his military uniform and knocked on the door. An elderly man opened the door. Pan Kapitan asked to see the Jewish boy who was living in the apartment. At first, the man denied having a Jewish child, But Pan Kapitan persisted and implied that he had information that a Jewish boy lived here. The man then decided to tell the story. He had been friendly with a couple, who worked for the Joint Distribution Committee in Warsaw prior to the war. The couple, named Barnowicz, had a boy and they wanted to save him. So they made an agreement with the Pole that he was to hide the boy in his apartment. They paid him and promised in writing that if the boy survived the war, the Joint Distribution Committee in the United States would pay additional compensation for the rescue of the child. The Pole even gave Drucker all the papers pertaining to the boy. The boy was told by the man never to approach the apartment window since his appearance was typically Jewish. The child did not listen and looked out from the window. The children below in the courtyard saw him and began to yell, "There is Jew in that apartment!" The Pole said that he was afraid for his life and chased the boy out of his place and onto the streets of Warsaw. Pan Kapitan informed the boy's uncle in Israel that he had found his nephew. The boy reached the kibbutz in Israel where he would grow up. He has returned several times to the farmer in Garbolin, Poland. He was no exception; most of the children who Pan Kapitan removed from non-Jewish homes eventually returned to visit the places where they lived during the war.

Drucker continued to devote himself to removing the Jewish children from non-Jewish homes. The task was getting more difficult by the day because the Polish government steadily increased full control of the streets and began to check all movements, including Zionist movements. The Polish secret services began to take an active interest in Jewish activities, including Jewish orphanages. The Central Committee kept pressuring the Polish government to take steps to limit all Zionist organizations and to prevent Jews from leaving for Palestine. Jewish emissaries from Palestine were checked prior to receiving permission to come to Poland. The Zionist homes slowly emptied by sending their residents out of Poland; even the Zabrze home made great efforts to send, legally or illegally, its young residents out of the country. Some Zionist homes and kibbutzim began to close for lack of new members and the elimination of the source of supply, namely the dwindling Jewish population in Poland. The Zabrze home was an official Polish institution under the auspices of the Polish army and was controlled by the Association of Jewish religious communities in Poland. The Central Committee of Polish Jews pressured Rabbi Kahana to integrate Zabrze with their homes. He dragged his feet, meanwhile taking all necessary steps to remove from the home as many orphans as he could and sending them abroad.

In 1948, the Zabrze home officially received an invitation to participate in the memorial services for the ghetto uprising of the Jews in Warsaw. This was indeed a surprise, for most of the participants belonged to groups that were close to the political regime. The home began to make extensive preparations for the event. Rehearsals were held and a delegation of children was selected to participate in the ceremonies, as well as an official delegation of the Zabrze home, and the Jewish community of Zabrze.

**The Zabrze official delegation to the memorial services for the Jews who revolted against the Germans. Zabrze official delegation headed by Dr. Nechema Geller. Behind her stands Rudolf Wittenberg, gym teacher of the Zabrze home, and to his left is Captain Drucker dressed in military uniform**

**Zabrze children waiting their turn to enter the parade in memory of the Jewish revolt in Warsaw**

Rabbi Kahana, now promoted to the rank of colonel, continued to protect the Zabrze home and his Association of Jewish Religious Communities. The Central Committee of Polish Jews applied pressure to out the Zabrze home under the wings of the Central Committee's education division. The pressure was relentless but Rabbi Kahana continued his independent path although he knew that his battle was lost. He soon decided to retire from the Polish army. The number of Jewish personnel in the Polish army had steadily declined and he began to plan to leave for Palestine. He planned to transfer the reduced chaplaincy office to Pan Kapitan. Also, Rabbi Aaron Becker decided to leave the Polish army. The chaplaincy office was thus reduced to one person, Pan Kapitan.

**Chaplain Aaron Becker, dressed in uniform, attends meeting of Mizrahi Zionist movement in Poland following the war**

As mentioned above, the Polish Communist government was slowly gaining control of the countryside. More and more police forces were created to cope with the lawlessness. The U.B. (*Urzad Bezpieczenstwa* or Polish secret police force) was greatly expanded and given large powers. The Polish Communist Party demanded action. Even the Central Jewish Committee of Polish Jews that was by now communist–dominated demanded immediate steps to prevent Jews from legally leaving Poland. It also demanded that the educational programs of the Jewish orphanages be realigned with the regular Polish school program. Rabbi Kahana used all his influence to delay the demands. The Polish government tightened control of Jewish legal emigration but permitted Jews to move to Palestine. The U.B. or Polish secret police began to follow Zionist activists. A significant change was taking place regarding Jews and Jewish organizations, especially those involved in Zionist activities. The Communist members of the Central Committee became vociferous in their demands that all Zionist activities throughout Poland cease. The Polish government took matters in hand.

The U.B. began to intimidate the Palestinian Zionist representatives in Poland. They were urged to leave the country. Leib Koriski, head of the Koordinacja office, or unified Zionist office for rescuing Jewish children, was placed under special surveillance. The Zionist homes tried to send all their children abroad. Zabrze was no exception. It expedited as many children as possible out of Poland. Below is a collective passport issued to a group of Zabrze children heading to Israel. Notice the stamps and the countries that they had to cross.

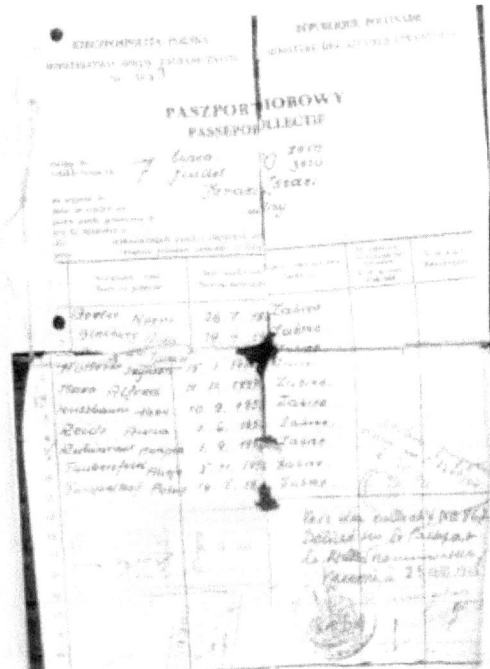

**Polish children traveling to Israel. All children listed were from the Zabrze home. They traveled via Czechoslovakia to Germany and France and then sailed to Israel.**

**Rabbi Kahana, second from left, leaves Poland from the port of Gdansk**

In 1949, Rabbi Kahane left Poland for Israel and managed to take with him some of the children. Upon his arrival in Israel he was appointed Chief Rabbi of the Israeli Air Force. Pan Kapitan replaced Kahana as Chief Chaplain of the Polish Army. He continued his activities in redeeming Jewish children but it became dangerous. Poland was becoming a communist dictatorship where movements were strictly controlled. Many checkpoints and road blocks were set up and traveling across the country became very difficult. The cold war atmosphere swept Poland. In 1948, Pan Kapitan was promoted to the rank of Major in the Polish Army. He met and married a Shoah survivor of Auschwitz, Miriam Wolfeiler, who worked at the Zabrze home. She gave birth to their daughter and named her Rachel, in honor of Pan Kapitan's mother.

Harsh police measures were soon enforced throughout Poland. Leib Koriski, Palestinian emissary and head of the Koordinacja office, was arrested and released on condition that he stop his activities in Poland. He continued his Koordinacja activities and was arrested again and interrogated. The police insisted that he provide evidence that all children who had left Poland had done so legally. While Koriski was in jail, Pinhas Kribus, another Palestinian emissary, was appointed to replace him. But the police hampered all activities of the Koordinacja office. Koriski was released and forced to leave Poland. All Palestinian officials in Poland were asked to leave the country. Rachel Sternbuch, who was a Swiss citizen, represented the Vaad Hatzala organization in Europe, especially in Poland. This organization was created by American Orthodox rabbis to help Orthodox rabbis and yeshiva students in Europe. She was also active on behalf of redeeming Jewish children from non–Jewish homes and institutions. She was arrested, kept in jail for a short period of time and then escorted to the border.

Active Jews were called to the police station and questioned. All were told that they were being watched. Even the members of the Bund or Jewish Socialist movement were being followed. The Bund was the best-organized movement in postwar Poland. It had a wide variety of institutions and branch offices in many cities in Poland. The organization frequently cooperated with the Communist Party in Poland. The Polish government decided to attack the Bund on two fronts. One way was to order the police to check and control the party activities. The Polish government also urged the Bund members to join the Polish Communist Party. The simultaneous pressure was too difficult to fight and the Bund decided to close its doors in Poland.

Most Bund members left Poland and headed to Australia, Europe, Argentina and even Israel, which they had so fervently opposed.

The Zabrze home was next in line. Pan Kapitan knew the days of independence were limited and there were still some children at the home. He managed to send some children with families that were leaving Poland. He also managed to place some other children with Jewish families in Poland. The staff was helped to leave Poland and the institution was closed. Pan Kapitan handed the keys of the home to the Association of Jewish Religious Communities.

**This document states that on "September 8, 1949, appeared before me Doctor Emilia Siliat Aleksandrowicz from the city of Gliwice. She officially adopted Sulamit Stefania Gottenberg from the nearby orphanage of Zabzre. The release from the orphanage was signed by Major in the Polish Army named Jezajasz Druckier Copy of adoption paper of Sulamit Gottenberg in Gliwice, Poland."**

Many Zionist officials began to leave Poland for Israel. Slowly but effectively, the Zionist political parties and their cultural institutions were forced to close their doors. The Jewish communities lost a good part of their Jewish population. Many Jewish activities stopped in Zabrze as the number of Jews steadily declined. Then on December 31, 1949, the Polish government informed the Joint Distribution Committee in Poland that it had to stop all activities on Polish soil. William Bein, head of the Polish office of the Joint Distribution Committee, tried to intervene but in vain. The decision shocked the entire Jewish community for the Joint Distribution Committee had extensively supported the Jewish communities and all Jewish institutions.

Institution after institution closed. This organization was also closed down by the Polish government.

Pan Kapitan retired from the Polish army as a major. The office of the army chaplaincy was closed in the Polish army. In 1950, Pan Kapitan, his wife and daughter left Poland and followed the children he had sent to Israel.

————

## Footnotes

1.  Drucker, Testimony, p. 65.

## Chapter XV

# Partial List of Children at Zabrze

These are children that appear in the album of Drucker. Many children did not stay at the home but were immediately released to relatives or adopted by Jewish families.

We do not know how many children Pan Kapitan removed from non–Jewish homes and institutions in Poland. He himself did not remember. He estimated between 600–800 children. Many of the children were removed from their Polish homes and immediately handed over to their Jewish relatives without staying at Zabrze, while others stayed at the home for a very short period of time and were never recorded. Pan Kapitan did not keep accurate records since most of his work was highly illegal and against the law being that he was a Polish officer on active duty. Still we have a substantial list of children that were registered at Zabrze. Their names appear below.

Most of the names appear in an album that Pan Kapitan assembled after he left Poland. The album with names and pictures was given to the museum of Lochamei Hagetaot where it can be seen.

| | |
|---|---|
| ADLER | Hela |
| AGART | Shmuel |
| AGART | Shmuel |
| AKIERMAN | Batia |
| AKRABSKA | Yanka |
| AKSELROD | Basia |
| ALMOG | Shimon |
| ALONI | Hana |
| ALTMAN | Yossef Tz |
| AUGMAN | Lillie |

| | |
|---|---|
| BENDER | Naomi |
| BERGMAN | Shoshana |
| BERLINSKI | Esther |
| BERNER | Lusia |
| BERNSTEIN | Simona |
| BLASSBERG | Ella |
| BLEIBERG | Dola |
| BORENSTEIN | Wira |
| BORENSTEIN | |
| BORENSTEIN | Zosia |
| BRANDES | Ryfwka |
| BRANDES | Ryfwka |
| BRENDER | Rivkah |
| BRENDER | Binyamin |
| BRENDER | Zwicka |
| BRESLAW | Nechema |
| BUKOWSKA | Stefa |
| CHALKES | Z |
| DANIELI | David |
| DANIELIM | David |
| DAWIDOWICZ | Ludyta |
| DIAMAND | Frida |
| DIAMAND | Paula |
| DINGOTLI | David |
| DITMAN | Dwora |
| DITMAN | Dwora |
| DOMB | Cesia |
| DRUKER | Ninka |
| ECKERT | Shmuel |
| EISENSTEIN | Batia |
| EPSTEIN | Aleksander |
| ETTINGER | Ewa |
| FALEK | Stasia |
| FALUCH | Irena |
| FELDMAN | Nehema |

| FENNER | Salomn |
|---|---|
| FISHBEIN | Henryk |
| FISZMAN | Marysia |
| FRAUEMGLASS | Klara |
| FRIEDLER | Eugenia |
| FRIEDMAN | David |
| FRIEDMAN | Dawid |
| FRIEDMAN | David |
| GESUNDHEIT | Samuel |
| GETTENBURG | Stefania/Shulamit |
| GLOWINSAKA | Roma |
| GLUTZENSTEIN | Eugenius |
| GOLDBERGER | Lea |
| GOLDFREIND | Hadassa |
| GOLDWASSER | Krysia |
| GORSKA | Lydia |
| GRIN | Chaika |
| GROSS | Niunnia |
| GROSSBERG | Helinka |
| HEFER | Michal |
| HEIMAN | Arthur |
| HEIMAN | Arthur |
| HERTZ | Miriam |
| HOFER | Sonia |
| HOFFMAN | Hanna |
| HOFFMAN | Jerzy |
| HOFFMAN | Hanna |
| HOTER–YISHAI | Yaakov |
| HUTTERER | Szymon |
| HUTTERER | Szymon |
| INBAR | Tz'ura |
| INDIK | Muszka |
| ISRAEL | Rivkah |
| JAKUBOWICZ | Basia |
| KAC | Jozef |

| | |
|---|---|
| KADER | Wita |
| KAFRI | Mordechai |
| KAGANOWIC | Liucia |
| KAPELI | Naumi |
| KAPUSZCIEWSKI | Yankel |
| KARNI | Marila |
| KASTENBAUM | Esther |
| KEVET | Orna |
| KLAINER | Inka |
| KLEINER | Inka |
| KLEINKOPF | Abraham |
| KLEINMAN | Hava |
| KLEINMAN | Eva |
| KLEINMAN | Hava |
| KLEINMAN | Eva |
| KOCZY | Florian |
| KOCZY | Hulda |
| KORN | Shlomo |
| KORNBERG | Mania |
| KOZOCH | Fela |
| LANDAU | Marin |
| LANDAU | Rita |
| LANDAU | Marin |
| LANDAU | Rita |
| LANDWIRTH | Danka |
| LANGBERG | Henryk |
| LAOS | Tusia |
| LEFKOWICZ | Riszard P |
| LEICHETR | Sara |
| LENCICKI | Aaron |
| LERER | Mina |
| LESLAU | Chana |
| LEV ARI | Hana |
| LEVANON | Rachel |
| LEWI | Halina |

| | |
|---|---|
| LEWITEK | |
| LIBMAN | Hava |
| LICHT | Leon |
| LICHT | Charlotta |
| LICHTENTHAL | Micia |
| LIVNA | Noa |
| LUBLINER | Adam |
| MAARAVI | Pnina |
| MAIER | Henryk |
| MAIZLISH | Hieronim |
| MARGEL | Hana |
| MARKS | Ruth |
| MASS | Celina |
| MATYL | Rivkah |
| MAYER | Heniek |
| MAYER | Sonia |
| MAYER | Heniek |
| MAZA | Alfred |
| MAZE | Alfred |
| MER | Djunia |
| METZGER | Joseph |
| MOTYL | Regina |
| NAJSRATER | Estera |
| NEBENTZAHL | Leah |
| NELSON | Hana |
| NEUBENFELD | Lipka |
| NEUMAN | Sabina |
| NIESSENTZWEIG | Ewa |
| NORTMAN | Sara |
| NUSSBAUM | Beni |
| NUSSBAUM | Abram |
| NUSSIMOV | Hava |
| PAKTOR–PICHOTKA | Batia |
| PEITZNIK | Jezik |
| PELED | Ilana |

| | |
|---|---|
| PIECZNIK | Jezik |
| PIOTERKOWSKI | Ryszard |
| PORILES | Ryszarda |
| PRIFER | Zenia |
| RADZIECHOWSKA | |
| REICH | Hannah |
| REUVANI | Lea |
| REUVEN | Yehudit |
| ROM | Djunia |
| ROMEK | Romek |
| ROSENBERG | Maria |
| ROSENBERG | Marysia |
| ROSENBLAT | Eduard |
| ROSENBLAT | Stanislaw |
| ROSENBLAT | Eduard |
| ROSENCRAC | Aliza |
| ROTHOLC | Ryszaed |
| ROZEN | Rozia |
| ROZEN | Rosia |
| ROZEN | Lila |
| RUBENSTEIN | Fania |
| RUBINRAT | Marysia |
| RUBINSTEIN | Halika |
| SAASIA | Miriam |
| SAASIA | Miriam |
| SADEH | Hana |
| SADEH | Moshe |
| SCHARK | Klara |
| SEIDEMAN | Basia |
| SEIDEN | Wisia |
| SERBERNIK | Danka |
| SHADMI | Chana |
| SHADMI | Chana |
| SHAEFFER | Shoshana |
| SHAFRIR | Hana |

| SHARON | Sara |
|---|---|
| SHEFER | Shoshana |
| SHEINFEKD | Batia |
| SHOR | Hanka |
| SHPIEGLER | Shlomo |
| SHPIEGLER | Zvi |
| SHPIEGLER | Shlomo |
| SHPIEGLER | Zvi |
| SHRAGGER | Rivkah |
| SHRAGGER | Rivkah |
| SHTERFELD | Arie |
| SHTERFELD | Arie |
| SILBERSHTEIN | Masha |
| SILBERSHTEIN | Masha |
| SNIADOWSKI | Abraham |
| SNIADOWSKI | Chune |
| SNIDOWSKI | Abraham |
| SNIGODOWSKI | Elhanan |
| SOBEL | Tzvi |
| SOBEL | Yehuda |
| SOBEL | Henryk |
| SOBEL | Tzvi |
| SPATZ | Dawid |
| SPIEGLER | Salomon |
| SPIRRER | Henryka |
| STEN | Ephraim |
| STIEGLITZ | Leon |
| STREIT | Felusz |
| STRUK | Danka |
| SWIATOWIC | Zipporah |
| SZERL | Ben |
| TAL–SHAHAR | Shaul |
| TAUBENFELD | Alicja |
| TAUBENFELD | Alicja |
| TAUBER | Majson |

| | |
|---|---|
| TEEEBAUM | Halina |
| TEMPELHOFF | Pavel |
| TEMPELHOFF | Pavel |
| TENENBAUM | Ilana |
| TILMAN | |
| TILMAN | |
| TOTENGRAEBER | Eliszewa |
| TZAPTER | Tzvi |
| UBMAN | Lillie |
| UBMAN | Lillie |
| ULKINDITZKI | Yehudith |
| WACHTER | Edzia |
| WAGNER | Madeleine |
| WAINMAN | Samuel |
| WALBERSTEIN | Moshe |
| WALD | Daniel |
| WALDHAMMER | Hanka |
| WALTUCH | Helena |
| WARSZAWIAK | Sara |
| WARSZAWSKA | Keysia |
| WASSERMAN | R |
| WATENBERG | Hana |
| WATTENBERG | |
| WEINLER | Andzej |
| WEINMAN | Wolf |
| WIENER | Sala |
| WILCZENSKI | Yehudit |
| WITUS | |
| WOHLHENDLER | Chawa |
| ZAIDMAN | Dawid |
| ZALCMAN | Alicia |
| ZALCMAN | Golda |
| ZAMTCHIK | Ella |
| ZAUBERMAN | Nina |
| ZAWARNICER | Ewa |

| | |
|---|---|
| ZILBERFEIN | Nusia |
| ZILBERMAN | Naomi |
| ZONENSHEIN | Rachel |
| ZONENSHEIN | Tzippa |
| ZONENSHEIN | Rachel |
| ZONENSHEIN | Tzippa |
| ZUCKERMAN | Abraham |
| ZUCKIERMAN | Salomon |

## CHAPTER XVI

# The Drucker Family in Israel

Pan Kapitan and his family left the port of Gdansk, Poland, and sailed to Haifa, Israel. Of course, he was not the only person to arrive in Israel. The country was flooded with Jewish refugees from Europe, mainly from the D.P. camps in Germany, Austria and Italy and also Jews from North Africa. The D.P. camps were being closed very rapidly.

Israel was not ready for such huge immigration. The country did not have the capacity to absorb such large numbers of people in such a short period of time. But the government could not stop the flow of refugees after it had kept repeating that the gates to Israel were open to all Jews and many of the Jews accepted the call and arrived in Israel. There were shortages of everything, mainly jobs and apartments. Nobody awaited Pan Kapitan at the port. All the people who had asked him for help in Poland seemingly disappeared overnight. He was left alone to face the difficult road of absorption. He had not established a strong connection to Israel and knew nobody of influence. All the people whom he helped ignored him. Even the head of the Jewish Agency Youth Aliyah department, Moshe Kol, refused to meet or extend help. Yet Pan Kapitan had sent hundreds of children to Israel with the help of Youth Aliyah. Drucker started to run around trying to get an apartment, which he finally obtained from the Jewish Agency in the city of Holon, south of Tel Aviv. Then he started to look for a job and found a clerical position with the help of an old acquaintance. Slowly and steadily Pan Kapitan and his family settled down in Israel. The absorption process was extremely difficult and frustrating.

By word of mouth, the news soon spread among the former Zabrze residents that Pan Kapitan has arrived in Israel. They slowly began to write letters and to visit him. The children were scattered all over the country. Some had adapted well to the country while others had great difficulties and problems. Pan Kapitan became the listener and solver of problems. He had their confidence and trust. In effect, he was their father and mother despite his own problems. The youngsters began to spent time with Pan Kapitan and received a great deal of attention that the society did not give them. To him they could talk in Polish and open their hearts and discuss their problems. His door was never closed. At times, he wondered whether he had done the right thing in taking these children out of their Polish homes and tossing them into the chaotic place of Israel where they had to swim on their own. Most of the children approved of his actions and were pleased to return to the Jewish fold. This gave him strength and confidence to continue to help the children.

**Moshe Kol**

Moshe Kol was born Moshe Kolodny on May 28, 1911, in Pinsk. He was one of the founders of the Ha–Oved Ha–Tzioni youth movement, a middle–of–the road Zionist youth movement in Poland. He immigrated to Mandatory Palestine in 1932. He joined the Histadrut trade union, serving as a member of its executive between 1941 and 1946, and also sat on the board of directors of the Jewish Agency, where he headed the Youth Aliyah department, that is, the illegal immigration of Jewish youngsters to Palestine. Pan Kapitan sent him many youngsters from Poland and received many requests from Kol to assist cases of children in non–Jewish homes. But Kol refused to lift a finger to help Drucker with his first steps in Israel. Pan Kapitan even wrote him a letter but Kol never answered. [1]

Pan Kapitan's family expanded in Israel with the birth of a son. The Drucker home became a beehive of activity for former residents of Zabrze, They came with problems and sought help. He listened patiently and answered their queries. According to former Zabrze orphanage resident Batia Akselrod Eisenstein, Pan Kapitan was both the father and mother that the children had lost in the war. [2] Most of the children adored him. He had collected photographs of the children at Zabzre and placed them in an album that he showed everybody. The album was later donated to the museum of the Lochamei Hagetaot at the kibbutz of the same name located near the city of Akko. Pan Kapitan considered the children as his children. He devoted all his energies to them and helped them with their many absorption and maturity problems. Michal Heffer, another resident of Zabrze, said, sitting in the living room of her Kfar Vitkin home, "I've made a good life in Israel." [3] Heffer is a published author and recognized artist in Israel. President Ezer Weitzman of Israel autographed one of her poems.

Ezer Weizman was born in Tel Aviv in the British Mandate of Palestine on June 15, 1924. His father, Yechiel, was an agronomist. Weitzman was a nephew of Israel's first president, Chaim Weitzmann. He grew up in Haifa, and attended the Hebrew Reali School. He married Reuma Schwartz, sister of Ruth Dayan, wife of Moshe Dayan, and they had two children, Shaul and Michal.

Weizman was a combat pilot. He received his training in the British Royal Air Force (RAF) and attended aviation school in Rhodesia. He served with the RAF in India in early 1944. Between 1944 and 1946, he was a member of the Irgun underground in Mandatory Palestine. Between 1946 and 1947, he studied aeronautics in Britain. He became commander of the Israeli air force and was later elected President of Israel.

The children of Zabrze showed their affection for Pan Kapitan by throwing a big party for him in the city of Holon where he lived. The party was attended by almost all former Zabrze residents in Israel. They continued to visit him even as he grew older, seeking paternal affection and compliments.

**Yeshayahu Drucker (with glasses) at a Zabrze Jewish orphans reunion, May 26, 1999, Holon, Israel**

**Former Zabrze residents at the home of Pan Kapitan**

**An aged Pan Kapitan surrounded by his devoted "children."
Reunion of former Zabrze residents with Yeshayahu Drucker. Standing from right
to left; Tziporah Domb, Fela Koshok, Hawa Klarsfeld and Shoshana Stein. Sitting
from right to left; Dawid Danieli, Yeshayahu Drucker and his wife Marioska**

Then the news spread throughout Israel that Pan Kapitan had passed away. He died on September 15, 2004. A year later, his wife Miriam passed away.

A gifted former resident of Zabrze, Michal Heffer, wrote this eulogy in Hebrew:

"קפטן דרוקר" היה איש אציל נפש, בעל שאר רוח, שמפעל הצלת הילדים היהודים מידי הנוצרים היה מפעל חייו.

לקפיטן דרוקר היתה עבורנו כל הסבלנות והאהבה לדם נזקקנו נואשות אחרי השואה האיומה. הוא היה המשפחה שלנו. אנחנו, ששרדנו יחידים בודדים ממשפחות שלמות, ראינו בו אח גדול. גם כשהיינו בצרפת, ממתינים לעלייה, לשם שלח אותנו על מנת להרחיקנו מפולין המסוכנת, כתבנו אליך, וכל מכתב התחיל ב: "אחי היקר". ואכן היה איש יקר, שהסתכן בלי גבול וללא כל חשבון עבור "ילדיו".

כשהלך להוציא ילד שלא תמיד רצה לחזור לחיק היהדות, או שמצילייו נקשרו לאותו ילד ולא אפשרו לו לעזוב, היה עליו לציתים לחטוף את הילד או לפנות לבית המשפט ובלבד להצילו! כשבא הרב דרוקר ביחד עם בן דודי, הסופר האידי יהודה אלברג, ז"ל, להוציא אותי מכפר פילציצה, ליד העיר קלצה, מעט אחרי הפוגרום שהפולנים ערכו ב-1946 ביהודים ששבו ממחנות ההשמדה, כמעט הרגו אותנו ביער, בדרך אל החזרה. רק תושייתו של הרב דרוקר הצילה אותנו.

עם זאת, לא פעם סיפר לי על הלבטים הקשים שהיו לו לקחת ילד מתוך קטן משפחה חמה אשר גידלה אותו מספר שנים כהוריו, מבלי שהיה מודע כי אינם הוריו האמיתיים, ולהעבירו לבית יתומים. או להוציא ילדה יותר גדולה ממשפחת מצילייה ולקרוע אותה שנית ממסגרת חייה על מנת להחזירה לחיק עמה.

היום אני יודעת את התשובה. פשיה נבון "קפטן דרוקר!". פעלת מתוך אחריות לאומית וגדלות נפש. אתה היית הקודרא'אק הפרטי שלנו, סמל ומופת!

כעת, כשהגעת לבית הדין של מעלה, שם בודאי הורו לך כשמגנו, ילדי ז'בז'ה, ובשם שאר הילדים שהצלת, מפני שעם ישראל הוא כאותו "עוף נחיל" המוזכר כבראשית רבה, י"ט, שנו כתוב: "עוף אחד ושמו חול'... אלף שנה הוא חי... ובסוף אלף שנה אש יוצאה מקינו ושורפתנו, ומותיר בו כביצה, וחוזר ומגדל איברים וחי".

אתה עזרת לנו לחזור, לגדל איברים ולהיות!

תודה לך קפיטן דרוקר.

תנחומינו לרעיתך מרים ולמשפחתך.

ינעמו לך רגבי עפרה של ישראל הקטנה, אליה שלחת אותנו לקיים חיים חדשים.

יהי זכרך ברוך.


מיכל חפר
כפר ויתקין, 15.10.04

## The translation of the Eulogy into English

Captain Drucker was a noble person endowed with a sensitive soul who immersed himself in the task of saving Jewish children from Christian homes. This endeavor became his raison d'etre. He had all the patience and love for us and we needed heaps of it following the Shoah. He was our family, we saw in him our big brother for we had no one to turn to, yet we all had large families that vanished during the war. Even when we left Poland, where we were in terrible danger and arrived in France, we continued to correspond with him. Our letters usually began with "dear brother." Indeed he was a dear man who risked his life for the sake of his "children." He frequently went on missions to extract Jewish children from Christian homes, knowing well that some of the children no longer wanted to return to the Jewish fold or the adopted parents refused to part with the child. Then Yeshayahu Drucker attempted to negotiate the release of the child. If negotiations failed he then resorted to the courts or even to strong–arm tactics in order to save the child. When Yeshayahu Drucker came with my uncle Yehuda Elberg, a Yiddish writer, to take me away from the village of Pilczica near Kielce shortly after the terrible Kielce pogrom of 1946 aimed at the surviving Jews, we were almost killed in the forest on our way to freedom. But thanks to the quick thinking of Yeshayahu Drucker we were saved. Yeshayahu Drucker frequently had moral doubts about his activities, for he realized that some of children had finally found a home where they were accepted. They had lived with the family for a number of years and frequently did not even know that these parents were not their biological parents. Then to come and break up the relationship was very painful. Furthermore, some of the children were older and even more sensitive to being traumatized again. But Yeshayahu was determined to save these children for the Jewish nation.

Now I understand your motive, Captain Drucker, you did it on behalf of the Jewish nation and sacrificed personal feelings. You were our Janusz Korczak, our standard bearer.

And now you will appear before divine judgment and you will be graciously thanked in all likelihood on behalf of all the children of Zabrze and all the other children whom you saved.

For the nation of Israel can be compared to that famous legendary bird of the sand that is mentioned in Genesis Raba, 19, where it is written "The bird lived for a thousand years, then it was consumed by fire but the remains provided the necessary elements for the rebirth of the bird." We are in the same situation, Captain Drucker, you have provided us with the necessary elements to grow again.

Thank you, Captain Drucker.

Our condolences to your wife, Miriam, and to your family. May the gentle soil of this small country accept you who has sent us to it to resume a new life.

May your memory be blessed forever.

Signed Michal Hefer
Dated October 15, 2004

*Translated from Hebrew by William Leibner*

**Pan Kapitan's resting place**

**The erection of a tombstone for Yeshayahu Drucker. Mrs. Drucker and daughter were present at the ceremony**

The children of Zabrze said goodbye to their adopted father who had cared and worried for them. They found in him a tower of strength as well as an ear. Yad Vashem organized two conferences where the former residents of Zabrze described the devotion of Pan Kapitan to the home.

**The happiest moments in Pan Kapitan's life was when surrounded by the children he saved and the staff**

**Pan Kapitan looking at the album with pictures from Zabrze**

**Jewish children saved by Yeshayahu Drucker and brought to Zabrze**

**Children at Zabrze stage plays**

**Children at Zabzre stage dances**

**Zabrze children hiking in the countryside**

**Reunion of former Zabrze orphanage children at Yad Vashem in Jerusalem**

-----

## Footnotes

1. Drucker, Testimony, p. 86.
2. William Leibner interviewed Batia Akselrod–Eisnstein
3. William Leibner interviewed Michal Heffer

## Chapter XVII

# Partial list of Jews of Jordanow

**The hamlet of Jordanow in the winter**

Yeshayahu Drucker was born in Jordanow and barely lived a number of months in the small hamlet. The family then returned to the city of Krakow. He never returned to Jordanow that later became a center for Zionist youth camps. The hamlet was badly damaged with the German invasion of Poland in September, 1939. Most of the local Jews were deported to the Belzec death camp where they perished. Jews were also killed by locals in large numbers. August 29, 1942, about 67 Jews were killed on the spot.

On August 29, 1942, about 67 Jews were killed on the spot.

## Partial list of Jews of Jordanow based on testimonies

| Last name | First name | Maiden name | Year of birth | Father | Mother | Gender | Husband |
|---|---|---|---|---|---|---|---|
| ABEL | Lonka | | 1912 | | | F | |
| BANDAMAC | Willi | | 1925 | | | M | |
| BANDAMAC | Samuel | | 1895 | | | M | |
| BANDAMAC | Roza | | 1893 | | | F | |
| BORENSTEIN | Shlomo | | | | | M | |
| BORENSTEIN | Gitel | | | | | F | |
| BORENSTEIN | Dawid | | | Shlomo | Giela | M | |
| BORENSTEIN | Tova | REIF | | | | F | Dawid |
| BORNSTEIN | Nuska | | | | | F | |
| BORNSTEIN | Dawid | | | | | M | |
| BORNSTEIN | Tova | | | | | F | |
| BORNSTEIN | Dawid | | | | | M | |
| BRAUNFELD | Nathan | | | | | M | |
| BRAUNFELD | Rachel | | | | | F | Nathan |
| BRAUNFELD | Hela | | 1900 | Nathan | Rachel | F | |
| BRAUNFELD | Sarah | | 1909 | Nathan | Rachel | F | |
| BRAUNFELD | Leibish | | 1911 | Nathan | Rachel | M | |
| BRAUNFELD | Giza | | 1905 | Nathan | Rachel | M | |
| BRAUNFELD | Abram | | 1900 | | | M | |
| BRAUNFELD | Gitel | | 1905 | | | F | |
| BRAUNFELD | Hershel | | | | | M | |
| BRAUNFELD | Priva | | | | | F | Hershl |
| BRAUNFELD | Genia | | | | | F | |
| BRAUNFELD | Miri Feig | | 1931 | | | F | |
| BRAUNFELD | Baruch | | 1933 | | | M | |
| BRAUNFELD | Reizel | | 1900 | | | F | |
| BRAUNFELD | Baruch | | 1933 | | | M | |
| BRAUNFELD | Rachel | | 1868 | | | F | |
| BRAUNFELD | Berka | | 1912 | | | F | |

| | | | | | | | |
|---|---|---|---|---|---|---|---|
| BURGER | Herman | | 1900 | Shimon | Khana | M | |
| BURGER | Yadviga | | 1901 | | | F | Herman |
| BURGER | Sara | | | | | F | |
| BURGER | Henia | | | | | F | |
| BURGER | Yisrael | | | | | M | |
| CYTERMAN | Friderika | | | | | F | |
| BURGER | Herman | | 1900 | Shimon | Khana | M | |
| BURGER | Yadviga | | 1901 | | | F | Herman |
| DONENFELD | Mendel | | | | | M | |
| DRUCKER | Israel | | | | | M | |
| DRUCKER | Rachel | | | | | F | Israel |
| DRUCKER | Yeshayahu | | 1914 | Israel | Rachel | M | |
| DUNKELBLUM | Simon | | | | | M | |
| DUNKELBLUM | Shmuel | | 1870 | | | M | |
| DUNKELBLUM | Gita | HABER | 1876 | | | F | Shmuel |
| EBERSTARK | Markus | | | | | M | |
| EINHORN | Malka | | 1901 | | | M | |
| EISEN | Max | | 1924 | | | M | |
| EISEN | Izaak | | 1924 | | | M | |
| EISEN | Chaja | | 1866 | | | M | |
| EISEN | Jakov | | 1923 | | | M | |
| ENDE | Yehoshua | | 1894 | | | M | |
| END | Mindel | | 1902 | | | M | |
| END | Zys | | | | | M | |
| ENGELHARDT | Lobl | | 1894 | | | M | |
| EBERSTARK | Markus | | | | | M | |
| EINHORN | Malka | | 1901 | | | M | |
| FORBER | Adela | | 1899 | | | M | |
| FRIEDHABER | Herman | | 1902 | | | M | |
| FRIEDHABER | Frida | | 1905 | | | M | |
| FORBER | Adela | | 1899 | | | M | |
| GELDZAEHR | Elimelech | | 1899 | | | M | |
| GELDZAEHR | Shimon | | 1886 | Chaim | Sara | M | |
| GELDZAEHR | Frida | | | | | M | Shimon |
| GLAZER | Adolf | | | | | M | |

| GLAZER | Felitzia | | 1898 | Shmuel | Roza | M | Adolf |
|---|---|---|---|---|---|---|---|
| GLAZER | Rachel | | 1897 | Zvi | Minda | M | |
| GOLDMAN | Jakob | | 1913 | Yossef | Chana | M | |
| GOLDMAN | Benik | | 1917 | Yossef | Chana | M | |
| GOLDFINGER | Baruch | | 1888 | Bernard | Roza | M | |
| GOLDFINGER | Amalia | WASSERBERG | | | | F | Baruch |
| GOLDFINGER | Baruch | | 1890 | Dov | | M | |
| GOLDFINGER | Malka | WASSERBERG | 1891 | David | | F | |
| GOLDMAN | Jakob | | 1913 | Yossef | Chana | M | |
| GOLDWASSER | Abram | | 1882 | | | M | |
| GOLDWASSER | Rywka | | | | | F | Abram |
| GOLDWASSER | Helen | | 1916 | Abram | Rywka | F | |
| GOLDWASSER | Hersh | | 1911 | Abram | Rywka | M | |
| GOLDWASSER | Izaak | | 1917 | | | M | |
| GRAU | Julius | | 1907 | | | M | |
| GRAU | Israel | | 1903 | | | M | |
| GRAU | Maurizio | | 1911 | | | M | |
| GRUBNER | Max | | | | | M | |
| GRUBNER | Tzipora | | | | | F | |
| GRUBNER | Max | | 1905 | | | M | |
| ISRAELOWICZ | Hana | | 1885 | Heinikh | Lea | F | |
| ISRAELOWICZ | Frida | | 1915 | Jakob | Hana | F | |
| ISRAELOWICZ | Sypra | | 1917 | Jakob | Hana | F | |
| ISRAELOWICZ | Yehuda | | 1925 | Jakob | Hana | M | |
| ISRAELOWICZ | Shmuel | | 1927 | Jakob | Hana | M | |
| ISRAELOWICZ | Heinikh | | 1930 | Jakob | Hana | M | |
| ISRAELOWICZ | Jakob | | 1885 | Don | Malka | M | |
| JUNGLEIB | Kaila | SCHECHTER | | Yossef | Adel | M | |
| JUNGLEIB | Eliezer | | | Menakhem | Kaila | M | |
| JUNGLEIB | Feige | KLAPHOLTZ | | | | M | Eliezer |
| JUNGLEIB | Berta | | | | | M | |
| JUNGLEIB | Pinkhas | | | | | M | |
| JUNGLEIB | Meir | | | | | M | |
| JUNGLEIB | Gabriel | | | | | M | |
| JUNGLEIB | Arnold | | 1903 | | | M | |

| | | | | | | | |
|---|---|---|---|---|---|---|---|
| GOLDWASSER | Abram | | 1882 | | | M | |
| GOLDWASSER | Rywka | | | | | M | Abram |
| GOLDWASSER | Helen | | 1916 | Abram | Rywka | M | |
| GOLDWASSER | Hersh | | 1911 | Abram | Rywka | M | |
| GOLDWASSER | Izaak | | 1917 | | | M | |
| GRAU | Julius | | 1907 | | | M | |
| GRAU | Israel | | 1903 | | | M | |
| GRAU | Maurizio | | 1911 | | | M | |
| GRAU | Zisl | | 1912 | | | M | |
| GRUBNER | Max | | | | | M | |
| GRUBNER | Tzipora | | | | | M | |
| KANNENGISSER | Ignatz | | 1900 | Shmuel | Regina | M | |
| KASNER | | | | | | M | |
| KAUFER | Chana | | | | | M | |
| KEGEL | Eliazer | | 1883 | | | M | |
| KEGEL | Chana | EIZEN | | | | M | Eliazer |
| KEGEL | Erwin | | 1912 | Eliazer | Chana | M | |
| KEGEL | Shmuel | | | | | M | |
| KEGEL | Rakhel | | | | | M | Shmue |
| KEH KAI | Debora | | 1898 | | | M | |
| KEH KAI | Hirsh | | 1901 | | | M | |
| KINSLINGER | Gitel | | 1901 | | | F | |
| KLAPHOLTZ | Jakub | | 1899 | | | M | |
| KORNFELD | Ignatz | | 1894 | Mendel | | F | |
| KORNFELD | Ana | FERSTER | | Markus | Rozalia | F | Ignatz |
| KORNFELD | Irena | | 1912 | Ignatz | Ana | F | |
| KORNFELD | Yehuda | | | | | M | |
| KORNFELD | Anna | | 1897 | Shimon | Feige | F | Yehuda |
| KORNFELD | Liber | | | | | M | |
| KORNFELD | Anna | DUNKELBLUM | 1892 | Shimon | Gitla | F | |
| KORNFELD | Yehuda | | | | | M | |
| KORNFELD | Anna | | 1897 | Shimon | Feige | F | Yehuda |
| KORNFELD | Yitzhak | | 1864 | Mendel | | M | |
| KORNFELD | Andza | | 1911 | Mordek | | F | |
| KRIGER | Leo | | 1902 | Shimon | Khana | M | |

| | | | | | | | |
|---|---|---|---|---|---|---|---|
| KRIGER | Hanka | | 1903 | | | F | |
| KRIGER | Khenekh | | | Shimon | Khana | M | |
| KRIGER | Helena | STANER | 1900 | | | F | |
| LILIENTHAL | Aron | | 1890 | Zigmund | | M | |
| ILIENTHAL | Hella | BURGER | | | | F | Aron |
| MARKUS | Hella | | 1925 | Abraham | | F | |
| MARKUS | Jakob | | 1920 | Abraham | | M | |
| MARKUS | Cilia | | | Abraham | | F | |
| MARKUS | Hinda | | 1885 | Mordechai | | F | |
| MUNK | Zalman | | 1919 | Israel | Malia | M | |
| NEUMAN | Malcia | | 1925 | Robert | Matilda | F | |
| REICHERT | Rana | | 1926 | Dov | Khaia | F | |
| STERNBERG | Awraham | | 1930 | Itzhak | Bela | M | |
| STERNBERG | Yitzhak | | 1891 | Menakhem | | M | |
| STERNBERG | Mindl | | 1857 | Yeshaya | Rakhel | F | |
| STERNBERG | Sijek | | 1926 | Itzhak | Bela | M | |
| STERNBERG | Bella | | 1884 | David | Miriam | F | |
| SZLAGIER | Yda | | 1905 | | | F | Lamek |
| SZLAGIER | Lamek | | | | | M | |
| SZWIMER | Frederyk | | 1904 | | | M | |
| SZWIMER | Olga | GOLDMAN | | | | M | Frederyk |
| TIMBERG | Beresch | | 1910 | Aharon | Rakhel | M | |
| TIMBERG | Adolf | | 1916 | Aharon | Rakhel | M | |
| TIMBERG | Cyla | | 1916 | Aharon | Rakhel | F | |
| TIMBERG | Zwi | | 1919 | Aharon | Rakhel | M | |
| TIMBERG | Jechil | | 1922 | Aharon | Rakhel | M | |
| TIMBERG | Beresch | | 1882 | Aharon | Rakhel | M | |
| WASSERBERGER | Liliana | | 1926 | | Sara | F | |
| WASSERBERGER | Wladyslaw | | | David | Jeti | M | |
| WASSERBERGER | Malka | GOLDFINGER | 1922 | David | Karola | F | |
| WASSERBERGER | Wadja | | 1996 | David | Karola | M | |
| WASSERBERGER | Sala | | | Shimon | Berta | F | Wadja |
| WILF | Heinrikh | | 1913 | | | M | |
| WILF | Berta | | 1915 | Adolf | Felitzia | F | |

# Chapter XIII

# Bibliography

Bogner, Nahum, Dr. Under the Mercy of Strangers, Yad Vashem 2000

Bauer Yehuda, Flight and Rescue , Random House, USA , 1970

Cichopek–Gajraj, Anna Beyond Violence, Cambridge University Press, 2014,

אחרי מות 'האם פעלנו למען הילדים.' העיתון הארץ, אורי דרומי. Hebrew

Drucker Yeshayahu, Testimony at Yad Vashem in Jerusalem. File # 10526, dated July 30, 1997.

Drucker Yeshayahu, Testimony at Yad Vashem in Jerusalem. Intervirw Tapes

Gutman, Israel, Jews in General Anders Polish Army in the Soviet Union, Reprint from Yad Vashem Studies, Vol XII, Jerusalem, 1977

1970, p.124 Yeshayahu Drucker's Tapes at Yad Vashem in Jerusalem, Israel

Jews in Walbrzych, Published in Poland by the Central Committee of Polish Jews. Polish

Kahane, David Rabbi, After the Deluge, Jerusalem, Israel, 1981. Pp. 10–14. Hebrew

Kahana, Rabbi David After the Flood, published by Mossad Kook 1981.

Kurtz David Aaron, The revival Story of the

Mizrahi and Hapoel Ha–Mizrahi movement in
Poland following the Shoa. Published by Book
Publishing Co., Israel 2002. Hebrew

Ouzan, Francois and Gerstenberger Manfred,
editors, Post war Jewish Disposition and Birth
1945–1947, Boston, Brill Publishing, 1967

Sarner, Harvey, Drugi Korpus Woyska
Polskiego, 1943–1947, Brunswick Press,1998

Turkov, Jonas En Pologne, après la liberation
(book was written in Yiddish "Noch dem
Bafraiung" and translated by Maurice Pfeffer
into French), published by Kalman–Levy in
2008

Yad Vashem –Pinkas Hakehilot

William Leibner interview with Orna Keret.

William Leibner interviewed Esther
Kastenbaum.

William Leibner interviewed Noah Livneh.

William Leibner interviewed Batia Eisenberg.

William Leibner interviewed Michal Heffer

William Leibner interviewed David Danieli

William Leibner interviewed Shlomo Korn

William Leibner interviewed Meir Weissblum

# INDEX

Please note that *this index does not include the names in the tables on pages 177 and 200*, so when looking for specific family names, please review these table separately.

www.ingramcontent.com/pod-product-compliance
Lightning Source LLC
Chambersburg PA
CBHW061835260326
41914CB00005B/1011